A Personal
Tour of Palau

WRITTEN BY ANN HILLMANN KITALONG
PHOTOGRAPHY BY WILLIAM E. PERRYCLEAR

Written & Published by:
Ann Hillmann Kitalong

Photographs by:
William E. Perryclear

Design & Layout by:
Margaret N. Mihlbauer
of Imagineering, Palau

ISBN 982-9041-06-9

For further information, send e-mail to
kitalong@palaunet.com

I dedicate this book to all my
family and friends.

TABLE OF CONTENTS

I began this book in January 1997. I said to myself, I will write on twenty topics. I will write one topic a week. If something comes up, I will stop for a while and pick up where I left off. Each topic was written separate from the other. There was no format or sequence at the time. Each topic describes some natural history and culture. Information was later checked from various sources. Any mistakes are my own. I appreciate your corrections (kitalong@palaunet.com). The main concept was that this was a personal perspective—how I see things. It does not mean that it is right or wrong—it is just how I see it. There is much factual information—the emphasis is my own. I highlight from my own experience or what I have learned through the years. My family and friends are the source of most of my information. So to them I am most indebted.

The sequence of the topics was later arranged to start with a brief history of Palau and then describe the marine ecosystems and activities including fishing, diving, the Rock Islands, marine lakes, canoes, rafts and kayaks, beaches and atolls. I ended with art and the traditional cultural center: the bai. My hope is to reach a wide audience of readers and deepen your appreciation of the ecological and cultural aspects of Palau. Throughout the text all Latin and Palauan words are italized. Definitions of Palauan terms can be found in the glossary at the end of this book.

This book includes the first ten topics of my efforts. The next book (coming soon!) will take us from the sea and reefs to the sea grass beds and mangroves. Then we will head to land and visit the taro patch—the most important activity for Palauan women. Other topics will include the streams, hunting in the forest and a visit to the waterfall and savanna. I will describe two important customs of birth and death from my perspective. I end with the clan, because the clan is very important.

This book is my attempt to scratch the surface of what Palau means to me. I hope that you see some of yourself between the lines.

Ann Kitalong

ACKNOWLEDGMENTS

My family shaped my life and this book. Clarence Kitalong, my husband and best friend, shared many adventures with me as well as his own childhood memories. Our family is molded by his creativity. My mother-in-law, Ngemelas Kitalong, lived in the days of sailing canoes and endured the hardships of World War II. She patiently continues to teach me. My sons, Clarence Jr. and Christopher show me life through their youthful and curious eyes. My mother, Mrs. Ann Keen Hillmann is the wind beneath my wings. My dad, Mr. Frederick Paul Hillmann taught me that hard work pays off. I live in a free and peaceful Pacific thanks to him and all the veterans who suffered and fought. My sister, Ms. Carol Jean Hillmann, did all the initial editing from Maine—through the magic of e-mail. She set up the first mock up and vision of this book.

Many friends made this book a reality. Bill Perryclear never gave up on me. Bill is the main photographer for the book. Inspired at a young age by the work of local Maryland photographer, A. Aubrey Bodine, Bill began a life long pursuit to capture images that are both fundamental and thought provoking. The text is brought to life through the eye of his camera. Bill has been a photographer all his life, as an amateur and then as a professional. The photographs not credited within the text are his.

Francis Toribiong taught me to dive over 20 years ago. Francis and Susan shared their passion for the sea with all of us. Susan Toribiong helped edit this book and gave helpful comments on farming. Margo Vitarelli reviewed and edited for me while sharing her insights on art, language, culture and life! Lynn Polloi read and shared her views with me over the years. Lynn, Margo and Sue are special friends. Maura Gordon reviewed my text and shared her insight on culture and fishing. Tina Rehuher gave helpful information on the bai and culture. Joshua and Simeon Eberdong shared tales of hunting and fishing over the years. Simeon Adelbai spent time reviewing slides and sharing his views on art and the bai. Nancy Barbour showed great enthusiasm for this project and was my very first reviewer. Mandy Thijssen-Eptison encouraged me and provided insight on canoes and culture. Nancy and Mandy warned me this would not be easy and they were right. Audrey Weinland and especially Bill Perryclear proofread and corrected grammar and provided helpful comments. Margaret Mihlbauer patiently designed and laid out this book and dealt with our never ending editing. I am greatly indebted to my family and friends. Thank you. You are all part of this book.

INTRODUCTION

From a distance Palau's main archipelago is shaped as a giant amoebae-like creature floating in the sea. A contrast of blues and greens outline the many islands and lagoons. A large reef narrows along the northern end of Babeldaob, Palau's largest island. Heading southward Palau widens to encompass lower Babeldaob and the Southern Lagoon.

The Republic of Palau is the westernmost archipelago in Oceania, an area encompassing Micronesia, Polynesia, and Melanesia. Palau is located at Latitudes 6° 53' to 8 ° 12' North and between Longitudes of 134°08' to 134° 44' East. The total area of reefs and mangroves is 1,940 square kilometers. A well-developed barrier reef system, about 112 kilometers (70 miles) in length and up to 32 kilometers (20 miles) wide, surrounds Koror, *Babeldaob* and Peleliu. Green lagoons lie in each direction. Especially well developed lagoons lie to the north and south. The archipelago stretches 700-km from *Ngeruangel* Atoll in the North to Helen Reef in the far South. The main islands stretch 150-km from *Ngeruangel* to *Angaur*. Palau has 8 large, 12 intermediate islands and over 500 small Rock Islands. These islands are part of an intricate system of fringing and barrier reefs.

The city of Koror on the island of Koror is the capital. In 2000, the population was over 19,000. The native language of Palauan is spoken throughout the islands. The native language and culture of the Southwest islands originates from the outer atolls of Yap. English is a well-spoken second language in Palau.

The total land area of Palau is 363 square kilometers. The largest island Babeldaob (332 square kilometers) is mostly volcanic. Terrestrial diversity includes more than 5,000 species of insects and 141 bird species representing 41 families and 16 endemic bird species. The native terrestrial mammals include two species of bats and one species of rat. Over 1200 species of plants are found in Palau of which over 100 are endemic including many endemic orchids.

Palau is renown world wide for its marine diversity. Thousands of marine species have been identified. Palau's diverse marine community includes at least 200 algae, 8 seagrasses, 100 sponges, 500 hard and soft corals, 250 mollusks (including the famous giant clams), 70 echinoderms, hundreds of crustaceans and other invertebrates and 1,500 fish species. Two species of endangered turtles, the hawksbill and green turtles are found in Palau. The most endangered marine species is the marine mammal, the dugong.

This is a conservative estimate of plants and animals in Palau. New species are discovered each year. Overall, there are more than 10,000 species of terrestrial and marine plants and animals in Palau.

Palauans immigrated from various parts of Asia a few thousand of years ago. Remnants of pottery, stonework, mysterious terraces, stone monoliths and stone faces are still found throughout the islands. Their oral history is passed down through legends and chants. Unique rituals celebrate the important events of life: birth, accomplishments during life and death. Palauans depend upon their natural resources for food, shelter, medicine, transport and traditional customs. Throughout its history Palau has been influenced by Britain, Spain, Germany, Japan and the United States. Today their political system is based upon the American democratic system. Yet their own traditional system of rule prevails.

Throughout the year, the climate is hot (average 85° F ranging from 24°-31° C) and humid (over 80% humidity). The maximum elevation is 230 meters. Rainfall averages 370 centimeters per year. Heavy rainfall usually occurs during December and January. The driest months are often January, February, March and April when there is less cloud cover and rain. The prevailing winds are from the Northeast during December through April. Southwest monsoon winds occur during May to October.

The major airline is Continental Air Micronesia with flights from Guam and Philippines. The airport is located on *Babeldaob* in *Airai* State. Upon landing you need an entry permit or passport. There is a departure tax. The Palau Visitors Authority can provide updated information at the following e-mail address: pva@palaunet.com or vist their web site at www.visit-palau.com. The mailing address is: Palau Visitors Authority, Box 256, Koror, Palau 96940.

A Glimpse of the Past

Mysterious terraces, stone megaliths, remnants of pottery, stone money, shipwrecks, piles of shell and bone fragments are pieces of Palau's puzzled past. Archeologists date the origin of Palauan civilization back as far as 3000 BC or nearly 5,000 years ago. Palauans call the earliest period of their history the time of the gods *(Taem era chelid)*. Biblical stories of the Old Testament parallel Palauan legends of demi-gods and a great flood. Worldwide, myths depict both human and super human traits. Paintings on the crossbeams of meeting houses *(bai)* depict demi-gods, famous wars, romances and tragedies. During the eighteenth century, Europeans documented beam paintings and legends. The written language is now a powerful tool to help explain Palau's story. Important people and events steered Palau's position in the world. Palauans are a warring, competitive people with incredible spirit and strength.

Palauans believe that their ancestors were seafaring people who sailed from the Philippines, Asia (Indonesia and Malaysia) and New Guinea. We see Melanesian and European influences in Palauan art and cus-toms. In the last century, Spain, Germany, Japan and the United States have influenced Palauan culture. Palauans adopted new skills and customs. Palauans base their clan linkages upon migration patterns, marriages, and the fate of their ancestors and immigrants from afar. The population size fluctuated from 50,000 people (in the 1800's) to about 3,750 people (early 1900's) to about 19,000 people today. The bottleneck in population size created closer alliances between clans. Palauan society became stratified into higher and lower clans and divided by competing warring confederacies with shifting alliances. I will try to unfold a small portion of Palau's past, so you can begin to understand where Palau has been and envision where it may be heading.

Palau's history really started millions of years ago with its geologi-cal past. Forty million years ago (The Eocene Period) the Philippine and Pacific Plates met. The Pacific Plate moved underneath the Philippine Plate causing great physical force and pressure. Earthquakes cracked the earth open and volcanoes formed on the Philippine Plate. These volcanoes grew above the ocean. The Palau Islands were born. Reefs gradually formed around the islands. Over

Photo at right: *Badrulchau* stone monolith, *Ngarchelong* State, Palau. Origin and purpose of these huge carved stones is still unknown.

millions of years the Palau Islands gradually sank. (Palau was originally five times bigger than it is today!) The reefs grew faster than the islands sank. So, Palau has many reefs and lagoons that were once land. During this time, some parts of Palau sank while other parts lifted upward. The northern atolls formed after its volcanoes sank. The southern reefs lifted 300 feet above the sea. The legend of Palau's origin is as violent as its geologic birth.

Once upon a time, gods roamed the earth. There is an area of shallow sea between *Angaur* and Peleliu called *Lukes*. At *Lukes*, a giant clam *(kim er a Lukes)* gave birth to a shrimp like creature named *Latmikaik*. *Latmikaik* gave birth to three children: *Chuab*, *Ucherrerak* and *Tellebuu*. *Chuab* was different. He had a huge appetite. At first the villagers kept up with his enormous appetite. Then their food became scarce and the people feared *Chuab*. The village decided to destroy the giant boy by fire. As *Chuab* died, his body transformed into a woman. *Chuab's* charred body exploded and her body parts became Palau. The back formed the East Coast and the front the West Coast. *Chuab's* head became *Ngarchelong* and the neck became *Arrenged*. The groin became *Aimeliik*, a village where

Traditional Palauan sailing canoe.

Storyboard carving of the mythical giant "Chuab."

there is much rain. *Chuab's* stomach became *Ngiwal*, where villagers eat seven times a day. The abdomen became *Melekeok*. *Chuab's* knees became *Airai*. The burned legs formed the Islands of Koror, *Malakal*, *Ngarkabesang* and *Ngerudabel*. The Rock Islands are bits and pieces of *Chuab's* body. Palauans link traits of villagers with *Chuab's* body parts. One imagines *Chuab's* body when describing the shape of Palau's Islands.

Successful warfare brought wealth and power. Bounties of war were land, money, titles and slaves. These same bounties caused war. Famous warriors skilled in weaponry won battles. Instruments of war included a club made with shell *(olechodech)* and an axe made with metal *(otilech)*. Other weapons included an adze *(chebakl)*, a club *(olumud)* and a wooden paddle *(brotech)*. Valuable pieces of large money passed between districts during war. Allies received money after a successful defense or attack on an adversary. Women were a bounty of war. (Legendary women of *Airai* and other States took more active roles in warfare.) In some cases, chiefs paid women to stop wars. The defeated chief paid money to the victors. After payment, the invaders returned to their home village and sent men back to rebuild what they destroyed during the conflict. If a defeated chief did not pay, the

invaders declared the village or municipality as theirs. Villages were built on hilltops to avoid coastal assault and terraced to afford more effective defense. Frequent warfare occurred along the coasts. Palauans built reef rock barriers over the fringing reefs to prevent passage of war canoes *(kabekl)*. Today, remnants of these reef barriers occur along the fringing reefs of *Ngaraard's* East Coast.

Strategy was a crucial part of war. The elders taught young men about different types of leadership strategies and personal discipline (*rolel a kelulau* or the way of politics) to attain recognition and power. Leadership strategies included the following: to please with gifts and parties, to perform a seemingly impossible feat, to surprise and confuse, to make successful threats, to show sympathy and compassion or use quiet rationale. Actions were circumspect yet competitive. The art of war required planning, developing alliances, learning new techniques, developing new weaponry and training great warriors for battles. A chief's goal was to make his clan powerful and wealthy. In the 18th Century, clans became powerful by using foreign resources. The Paramount High Chief of Koror, Chief *Ibedul,* acquired skillful warriors and effective weapons including introduced firearms, to win his battles. Although a great friendship developed between Chief *Ibedul* and British Captain Wilson, usually Palauans feared and distrusted foreigners.

Allies were crucial in war. Strong and united clans won battles. Palauans held large dance parties between friendly villages

Palauan money beads resting in turtle shell tray known as *"toluk."*

that lasted for months. These parties strengthened relationships. Villages reciprocated favors by assisting in battles and community activities like building a community *"bai"*. Knowledge was a key to power. Chiefs were alert to shifts in alliances or signs of discontent.

Color pencil drawing by Palauan artist John Q. Demei depicts Palauan war canoe of the past.

The cause of a war was basic: to gain power or wealth or to take revenge for a previous defeat. Chiefs encouraged young men to raid villages. A war party only needed to kill one man to be victorious. Chiefs ordered short raids to obtain money for themselves and the men's clubs. A siege was a large and more complex battle to establish new alliances and distribute wealth. Most wars were skirmishes rather than full-scale battles. Chiefs sent messengers to a village they planned to raid. The messenger provided the challenged village with a list of their war canoes and men. If the council of chiefs of the challenged village knew they would lose, they simply made a payment to the challenging chief and no battle took place. However, if they decided to accept the challenge the war proceeded. The challengers first made a show of their strength. Then a few warriors approached the villages. The first side to lose a warrior lost the battle. Historians can recite the major battles and heroic warriors of their villages.

Palauan legends describe the earliest battles between demigods and gods. One legend is about a time of conflict between *Ngiwal* and *Ngaraard*. *Ngiwal* had a string of victories. The *Ngaraard* warriors could not defeat the great *Ngiwal* warrior, *Uchel*. Then, one day a *Ngaraard* woman noticed a shore bird catching fish while walking along the shore. She saw the bird take two steps before it made a final third step to catch its prey. The bird never missed. She decided to share this hunting technique with her son, *Rechemechem*. He watched the bird's technique and practiced it with his spear. Soon *Rechemechem* never missed his target. During the next battle, *Rechemchem* easily speared *Uchel* and *Ngaraard* was victorious. *Rechemchem* became *Ngaraard's* hero.

One of the greatest warriors of Palau was *Ngirngemelas* of *Ngiwal*. There are at least three legends about *Ngirngemelas*. During his time, *Ngaraard* was again at war with *Ngiwal*. *Ngaraard* had a string of victories and *Ngiwal* was losing their men. *Ngaraard's* warriors killed boys and men. As a young boy, *Ngirngemelas* was sent to *Airai* to learn the art of warfare. He lived and trained with the *Debkar* clan. A tall, athletic and intelligent young man, he learned quickly and became quite skillful in the various disciplines of combat. Soon he would face the treacherous journey to return to his native village of *Ngiwal* for at the time there were marauding bands of

Prince Lee Boo, Palau's first ambassador to the outside world.

warriors from competing villages who killed young men of warrior age. *Ngirngemelas* developed an ingenious disguise to facilitate his return. At the time, leprosy was a common disease in Palau and those so infected were considered outcasts and isolated from the rest of the society. In order to appear a leper, *Ngirngemelas* allowed sores to fester on his body. To enhance his disguise, he tied rotting fish to his ankles which created an overpowering stench that kept people at a distance.

His clever disguise permitted him to return, uneventfully, to his village. When the time was right, *Ngirngemelas* finally led *Ngiwal's* warriors into victory. Under his heroic leadership, *Ngiwal* continued to be victorious over *Ngaraard*. Another legend about the famous *Ngirngemelas* describes his triumph in Peleliu. One day, *Obirir*, a woman of Peleliu, came to *Ngaraard* and asked *Ngirngemelas* to help defeat *Angaur*, Peleliu's relentless enemy. *Ngirngemelas* agreed. To *Obirir's* delight, the *Angaur* warriors were no match for *Ngirngemelas's* strength and cunning. *Ngirngemelas* married *Obirir* but later returned to *Ngiwal*. In a third legend, Palauans portray *Ngirngemelas* as a compassionate man. A man named *Ngirailemesang*, from the neighboring village of *Ngkeklau*, was not a brave man in battle and was unable to find a wife. Desperate to obtain some prestige in his village, *Ngirilemesang* asked *Ngirngmelas* to permit him to just spear the warrior's foot. *Ngirailemesang* promised him a good payment and the necessary healing medicines. *Ngirngmelas* agreed. *Ngirailemesang's* ploy worked. He speared the warrior's foot; he gained prestige and married. Today, the people of *Ngiwal* still revere their legendary hero. Their welcome sign proudly reads "The home of *Ngirngemelas*."

Palauans describe another cunning hero in the famous legend called *"Bekeu el Bngaol."* Once upon a time there was a war between *Ngeremlengui* and *Ngarchelong*. One

night, the *Ngeremlengui* warriors (124 men) paddled in their war canoes to capture one man from *Ngarchelong*. *Ngeremlengui* surprised *Ngarchelong* and easily captured the man they sought. In darkness, they paddled home through a mangrove channel *(taoch)*. Along the way, their captive saw a low-lying branch of the mangrove tree, *Rhizophora apiculata (bngaol)*. As the canoe approached the low branch, he slowly raised his hands above his head. While passing the branch, he quickly grabbed it and pulled himself upward. Nobody noticed his escape! Meanwhile, the *Ngarchelong* chiefs gathered to discuss their rescue strategy. As they spoke, the escapee slowly walked into the village. Surprised, they ran to him and asked what happened. They listened to his story and celebrated his success. Palauans call the place of his escape *"Bekeu el Bngaol"* or "the fighting mangrove tree."

These few legends illustrate how Palauans valued their warriors for bravery, cunning, compassion and the ability to create new strategies. There are many legends about famous battles and war heroes of Palau. Several legends show how women both directly and indirectly affected the outcome of battles. When European ships came to Palau, traditional warfare and its culture began to experience change. At first, changes were few and subtle.

In the mid-1500's, Palauans sighted Spanish ships. On October 3, 1579, while en route around the world, the English adventurer, Sir Francis Drake, traded briefly with Palauans of *Babeldaob* (Palau's largest island.) The bounty of his ship tempted the overwhelmed Palauans to steal.

Plaque on monument at *Ulong* Island commemorating the shipwreck of Capt. Wilson's ship, the ANTELOPE, on August 9, 1783.

Sir Drake's men fired shots into the air and Palauans threw spears from their canoes. No one was hurt during this unpleasant encounter. Two hundred years passed until records described several ill-fated Spanish ventures to Palau. In the Philippines, Father Klein took a keen interest in Palauans who accidentally drifted there during storms. In 1697, Father Klein influenced the Jesuit General of Rome to expand Christianity to the "Palaos" Islands. After several unsuccessful attempts, the "Santissima Trinidad" commanded by Don Francisco de Padilla, left the Philippines for Palau. This ship sailed for both religious and political interests. In December 1710, "Santissima Trinidad" landed at *Sonsorol* Island of the Southwest Islands of Palau and the islanders warmly welcomed them.

Two Flemish priests, Fathers Duberon and Cortil decided to overnight on *Sonsorol* and erect a cross. During the night, Francisco de Padilla was unable to secure his ship against the strong currents and had to leave the priests behind. The ship sailed North, went through the channel between Peleliu and *Angaur* and headed to *Babeldaob* and then headed back to the Philippines. A year later another ship tried to return for the priests but a storm intervened. Some thought that the natives killed the priests soon after their arrival. On February 12, 1712, Captain de Egui commanding a Spanish ship finally returned to Palau. Upon the ship's arrival, violence broke out between the crew and the natives. Several Palauans and a crewmember died. The Spaniards captured two Palauans but they escaped. The

attitude of conquest rather than cooperation and exchange may explain Spain's early failure to trade with and convert Palauans. For the next 75 years, there were no records about foreign ships in Palau.

The most famous shipwreck in Micronesia occurred the night of August 9, 1783. While en route to Macao, the stormy seas lifted the British packet, Antelope, onto a western reef near *Ulong* Island, Palau. This packet ship of the East India Company was a passenger boat that carried mail and cargo on a regular schedule. The commander, Captain Henry Wilson of London, ordered the mast cut so the ship did not capsize. The crew of 50 men including 15 Chinese, salvaged what they could from the wreckage and transported it to nearby *Ulong* Island. They set up camp and began to rebuild a ship to carry them to Southeast Asia. Within two days, the Paramount Chief of Koror, Chief *Ibedul* sent his two brothers and a castaway named Soogle to meet Captain Wilson.

Chief *Ibedul's* assistant, Soogle was fluent in Malay and Palauan. Captain Wilson's linguist, Tom Rose was fluent in Malay and English. When Soogle called out to the shipwrecked crew, Tom Rose responded. Tom Rose translated Malay into English for Captain Wilson. Soogle translated Malay into Palauan for *Ibedul's* brothers. The ability to communicate enabled Wilson and the *Ibedul's* men to understand each other. Captain Wilson invited them for tea and biscuits and asked for their help. Chief *Ibedul's* brothers liked the biscuits and other new items. They realized that Captain Wilson was indeed in need of their help. Captain Wilson sent his brother, Matthias, to meet Chief *Ibedul*. Five days later, Chief *Ibedul* arrived with his son *Lebuu* and a fleet of war canoes and 300 men. Captain Wilson graciously welcomed Chief *Ibedul*. He gave Chief *Ibedul* a ham, a goose and an officer's uniform. In return, Chief *Ibedul* offered his protection and sent canoes loaded with food for

Wilson's crew. Wilson introduced many new things to Palau. He carried dogs and geese aboard his ship, animals never seen before by Palauans. Ancient pictographs painted on the cliffs of *Ulong* island show the figure of a dog. Iron, bronze and other ferrous metals were first brought to Palau aboard the Antelope. Having no

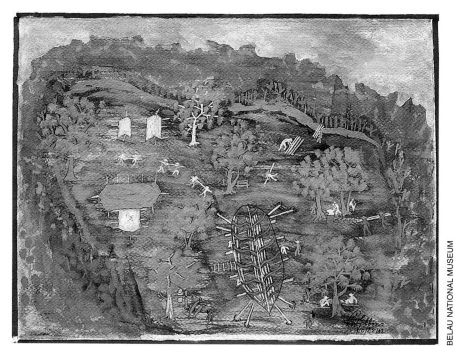

Charlie Gibbons painting of the rebuilding of the ANTELOPE on *Ulong* Island.

BELAU NATIONAL MUSEUM

knowledge of metals, the natives watched with great interest as Wilson's blacksmith heated, bent and shaped various metals into useful tools and weapons. A mutual understanding and trust developed between Chief *Ibedul* and Captain Wilson that lasted a lifetime.

Firearms were on board the Antelope. The crew demonstrated the power of firearms to Chief *Ibedul* and his men. The British were unaware that firearms would change the traditional balance of power in Palau.

Within seven days of landing on *Ulong* Island, Chief *Ibedul* asked Captain Wilson to assist him in battle with *Artingal* (the district of *Melekeok, Ngchesar* and *Ngiwal*). The indebted Captain Wilson agreed. British crewmen fought in several victorious battles supporting the causes of Chief *Ibedul* thus making Chief *Ibedul* the most powerful man in Palau. Before Captain Wilson's arrival, chiefs relied upon alliances with other villages during

CHAPTER 1: A HISTORY OF CONFLICT

10

A PERSONAL TOUR OF PALAU

warfare with more powerful opponents. Single villages seldom had sufficient manpower, resources or political clout to take on the likes of *Peleliu* or *Artingal* single handedly. In the first engagement against *Artingal*, six British sailors joined Chief *Ibedul's* warriors in five different canoes. The entire war party was made up of 150 canoes and more than 1000 men. An Englishman fired only one shot that killed an *Artingal* warrior. Koror was victorious. Chief *Ibedul* demanded his bounty of war from Chief *Reklai,* the Paramount Chief of *Artingal*.

Chief *Reklai* did not meet his obligations from the first battle with Chief *Ibedul*. So Chief *Ibedul* ordered a second battle. This time, Chief *Ibedul* sent 10 British sailors and 200 canoes of warriors to attack *Artingal*. Chief *Ibedul's* men captured and wounded more of Chief *Reklai's* men than during the first battle. Koror warriors executed nine wounded captives on the spot. The British felt the executions were unduly cruel. On October 3, 1783 a third battle with *Artingal* took place. This time, the firearms of Koror did not surprise *Artingal* whose warriors fought with determination and courage. During the long battle, 30 to 40 of Chief *Ibedul's* men were seriously wounded, some mortally. It was only through the superior fire power of British muskets and a swivel gun mounted on the front of a canoe that the forces of Koror's Chief *Ibedul* were able to prevail. The Paramount High Chief of *Artingal*, Chief *Reklai*, finally accepted defeat. Chief *Ibedul* confiscated Chief *Reklai's* special stone bracelet *(btangch)* and destroyed *Artingal's* causeway. A fourth battle against Peleliu *(Belilou)* never

Yapese stone money quarried in *Airai* State, Palau.

occurred. Upon arrival, Koror found a deserted village and declared victory.

On November 12, 1783, three months after their shipwreck, Captain Wilson's crew completed their new, smaller ship, *Oroolong* (named after *Ulong* Island). Captain Wilson prepared to depart for Portuguese Macau. One crewmember wanted to stay in Palau. Chief *Ibedul* wanted the crewmember to continue training his warriors about firearms. Captain Wilson left firearms and ammunition with Chief *Ibedul*. As a parting gesture, Chief *Ibedul* presented him with a dugong bracelet. (This bracelet is one of the vertebrae of the marine mammal, *Dugon dugong*.) Chief *Ibedul* sent his second son, *Lebuu,* with Captain Wilson. Chief *Ibedul* wanted *Lebuu* to learn from the British and then return to Palau.

Captain Wilson took great honor in having *Lebuu* in his care. The British called him Prince Lee Boo and this young man (perhaps 19 or 20 years) represented Palau with grace and charm. Britain adored Prince Lee Boo, who adapted well to the customs of their country. Six months after his arrival to Britain, Prince Lee Boo became tragically ill with smallpox and died on December 27, 1784. Captain Wilson buried Prince Lee Boo at his family gravesite in the cemetery of St. Mary's church. A poem inscribed on the tombstone reads, "Stop, Read, Stop! - Let Nature claim a Tear. A Prince of Mine Lee Boo lies bury'd here." In Britain, George Keate wrote a bestseller called, "An Account of the Pelew Islands." Mr. Keate referred to Captain Wilson's personal journal and described accounts of his shipwreck. Keate's book brought enduring fame to

Palau and Prince Lee Boo. In London there is a gravesite marked in honor of Prince Lee Boo that can be found on Rupak Street. Today, Palauans travel to England and visit the gravesite of Prince Lee Boo.

In 1791, seven years later, Captain McCluer and Captain Drummond returned to Palau to inform Chief *Ibedul* of his son's death. Despite the sad news, Chief *Ibedul* warmly greeted and exchanged gifts with the ship's Captain. The British brought Chief *Ibedul* cows, bulls, boars, sheep, goats, ducks and geese.

Sacred Heart Church. The Catholic Church was established in Palau in 1891.

Chief *Ibedul* asked McCluer's crew to help during three raids. During one raid the British showered *Artingal* with Chinese rockets and fireworks that led to immediate surrender. Chief *Ibedul* received more Palauan money and 60 women as hostages to serve in Koror's men's club-houses.

Sailing ships of whalers and traders began to frequent Palauan waters. Between 1710 and 1798, records document eleven ships voyages in Palauan waters. Between 1800 and 1891, records list seventy-three foreign ships visited Palau. The recorder, James Gibbons, was a Jamaican-English immigrant, whom Chief *Ibedul* appointed administrator of Koror. Whalers simply wanted a safe port and provisions. They traded iron for provisions and spent a short time in Palau. Traders established trading posts, homes and interacted regularly with Palauans. Foreign relationships changed from mutual friendship to hard bargaining. Palauans and foreign parties felt no indebtedness towards each other. Palauans learned the value of their natural resources and what constituted a

good quality import. The British thought Chief *Ibedul* was monarch of all Palau. Foreigners did not understand that Chief *Ibedul* was one of many chiefs and not the only paramount chief in Palau. Chief *Reklai* was the paramount chief in *Artingal*. In addition, Chief *Ibedul* had to consult with other chiefs of Koror before he could finalize important decisions for Koror. This misconception and Chief *Ibedul's* cunning helped Koror become the most powerful district in Palau. Today, Koror remains the business district of Palau.

A Scotsman named Andrew Cheyne (1791-1883) was the most influential trader in Palau in the eighteenth century. Cheyne first arrived in Palau in 1843 and his last recorded voyage was in 1866. Cheyne made three voyages with his ship, Black River Packet, and six voyages with his ship, Acis. Cheyne traded iron, tobacco and guns with Koror. He bought *Malakal* Island (*Ngemelachel* Island) from Chief *Ibedul* where he processed sea cucumbers, coconut oil and turtle shells. Another trader, Captain Edward Woodin, an Englishman from Tasmania, competed with Cheyne. Woodin established a trading post in *Ngebuked, Ngaraard.* Cheyne naturally opposed Woodin's trading post because it competed with his trade. He successfully persuaded Chief *Ibedul* to support him. In 1861, war broke out between Chief *Ibedul* and Chief *Madrengebuked* of *Ngaraard*, who supported Woodin. During the battle, a brave warrior, *Rechelulk* (who later became Chief *Madrengebuked*) with a cannon bearing canoe, sank one of the war canoes causing Koror to retreat. Thus Woodin continued his trading post in

Ngaraard. By 1865, Cheyne began plantations (sugar, coffee, cotton, bananas and indigo) in *Babeldaob* with Chinese laborers. Palauans eventually killed Cheyne. Perhaps Cheyne became too greedy with their natural resources. Captain Stevens, a representative of the British government came to investigate the murder. Stevens' records state that his men shot Chief *Ibedul.* Authorities of Palau tradition believe that the British really shot Chief *Rechucher,* another high clan chief of Koror, who posed as Chief *Ibedul.*

The tide was beginning to turn for Koror's dominance in power. Warfare was becoming more challenging and the victors less predictable. In 1868, Captain Tetens (originally commanding Cheyne's ships) joined forces with Chief *Ibedul* to battle against *Artingal.* Koror's armada included eight large war canoes and sixty to seventy sailing canoes with European and Malayan troops. During the battle, *Artingal's* warriors wounded Captain Tetens in the leg, causing Koror to retreat. Meanwhile other factors came into play. *Kayangel* attacked Koror by surprise and took back their female captives from a previous battle. Chief *Ibedul* retaliated. He chartered a Spanish schooner, Rosario, to sail to *Kayangel.* Koror's warriors killed seven men in *Kayangel* and captured the rest.

In 1871, Johann Kubary, a Polish ethnologist working for the Godeffroey Museum in Germany, arrived in Palau. During a flu epidemic in 1872, Kubary successfully treated sick patients and gained respect from the Koror community. Kubary's wife was a Pohnpeian named Yelirt. Eventually, Kubary went to *Artingal* to live. Kubary's writings were an important contribution to Palauan history and culture during the 19th century.

An Irishman, David Dean O'Keefe was the most famous trader in Palau. O'Keefe left his home in Savannah Georgia after being convicted for the murder of two of his crew. O'Keefe's ship went aground in Yap. O'Keefe, the sole survivor, set up a base in Yap and began trading in the Western Carolines in the 1870's. At the time, as is the case today, Yap and Palau were closely related through geographical proximity, and similarities in their culture. In the days of O'Keefe, the Yapese sailed to Palau to quarry aragonite, a kind of limestone commonly found in the Rock Islands. Huge pieces of aragonite were chiseled from cliff faces and fashioned into circular plates. Some were more than 10-feet in diameter, 3-feet thick and weighed several tons. These huge stones were of immense value in Yap as a result of the difficulties endured in their manufacture in Palau and subsequent shipment to Yap. The many lives lost while transporting them over 300 miles of open ocean on sailing canoes and rafts only served to increase their value.

Seeing the difficulties encountered by the Yapese in bringing these large pieces of "money" back to Yap and wishing to ingratiate himself with the powerful and influential men in both Yap and Koror, O'Keefe

Remnants of Japanese Era pineapple canning plant near *Ngeremlengui,* Palau.

offered the services of his ship. By 1881, the Yapese mined over four hundred stone monies in Koror. Today, the Yapese money quarried before O'Keefe's trading business is more highly valued due to the hardship and deaths during Yap's traditional journeys.

In *Babeldaob*, hostility grew as a result of O'Keefe's lucrative and exclusive trade of Yapese money and imported goods with Koror. O'Keefe's ship, Lilla went aground between *Ngetelngul* and *Ngarchelong*. Warriors plundered his ship and mistreated his crew. As a

Bauxite mining terraces, *Ngardmau* State, Palau.

result of this incident, a dispute began between Koror and *Melekeok (Artingal)*. Britain sent Commander Cyprian Bridge to resolve this dispute. On August 11, 1883, after years of constant conflict, Chief *Ibedul* of Koror and Chief *Reklai* of *Melekeok (Artingal)* signed a peace treaty, putting an end to inter-village warfare.

A legend describes the last traditional Palauan war. This war was between *Aimeliik* and *Airai* in 1885. A brave warrior named *Olikes* was the leader of *Ngarateleber,* a men's club (*cheldebechel*) of *Aimeliik*. With the introduction of firearms, *Olikes* knew traditional Palauan warfare would soon end. He wanted to lead his men in the last Palauan war. *Olikes* learned that the *Ngaramekebud* (men's club of *Airai*) gathered at the *Ngerbuud "bai"* in *Ngeruluobel*. They were in the company of their female companions of the *"bai."* That night, *Olikes* and 34 members of *Ngaratelber* invaded *Ngaramekebud* in *Ngeruluobel* Village of *Airai*. *Olikes's* men attacked with guns (*skobetang*), spears and battle-axes. The sudden attack caused a state of confusion in the *bai*.

Ngaramekebud's men picked up their guns and randomly fired at the roof. Meanwhile the clay lamps (*olbidl*) used to illuminate the *bai* continued to burn. *Dind*, a concubine (*mongol*) from Peleliu, quickly extinguished the lamps. Once the light was out, the panic ended and *Olikes's* men fled. The *Ngarateleber* men suffered only minor injuries during the attack. (An arm injury to one man, *Ngiratangergoi*, was the most severe.) Two months later, *Ngaramekebud* sent four men on a reprisal raid under the leadership of Captain *Kiukl*. (At this time, Palauans used the term "Captain" to refer to their leader.) Captain *Kiukl* captured and beheaded *Olikes*. The warriors brought back *Olikes's* head to *Airai* as proof of his death. The severed head of an enemy or victim of revenge is called *"lebaol."* The *Airai* community celebrated with the triumphant raiding party (*mengituuk*) and the time of traditional warfare ended.

The Spanish period (1885-1899) was a time of international rivalry and missionary effort. In 1885 Pope Leo XIII issued a papal bull granting sovereignty of the Western Caroline Islands to Spain but gave commercial rights to Germany and Britain. The Germans established a naval station, mined phosphate and began agriculture projects during the Spanish period. Spain was not a strict administration. In June 1886, the Spanish Capuchins (Capuchins are a Catholic religious order) came to open a mission. In July 1890, Fr. Daniel Arbacegui, the Capu-

Photo at right:
German Channel, built during the
German Administration.

chin Superior in Yap, and a lay brother, Antolin Orihuela, sailed to Palau aboard O'Keefe's trading schooner, the Santa Cruz. In April 1891, the Santa Cruz again came to Palau with four Capuchins, two priests and two brothers, who founded the first permanent missionary.

The Capuchins waged a religious battle against female entertainment in the clubhouses *(klomengelungel)* and other cultural practices such as the ease of divorce and remarriage, local sorcery and spirit communication. During 1892, an epidemic of influenza broke out in Palau. The Capuchins helped the sick and established more credibility to their religion. Yet, an ongoing religious battle continued. The older Catholic community recalls the ill fate of the Spanish Capuchin, Father Luis de Granada. In1893, *Ngarchelong* villagers became frustrated with Father Luis's chastising. They tried to deter him by building his house with the tree, *Spondias pinnata (titimel),* a wood that rots easily. Worse yet, in *Chelab, Ngaraard,* the villagers smeared human excrement on the church altar where Father Luis offered services. The frustrated Father Luis left *Ngaraard* and moved to *Ngiwal* with the support of Chief *Reklai* of *Melekeok.* In 1903, Father Luis moved to *Melekeok,* where the villagers deliberately sent him in the wrong direction while traveling in *Ngchesar.* Eventually,

This structure, located at the dock in *Ngardmau,* was part of the bauxite mining operation. Bauxite was transported to the dock by gondolas.

Father Luis passed away and the people buried his body on Chief *Reklai's* grave. They marked his grave with coral, to indicate that he came from across the sea. Father Luis' efforts resulted in a small mission in *Melekeok* that became Christianity's foothold in *Babeldaob.*

On December 10, 1898, Germany bought the Carolines, Palau and part of the Marianas from Spain for 18,000,000 deutsche marks (US $4,500,000). The Germans administered Palau from 1899 to 1914. Initially, the German administered from their base in New Guinea. Ships delivered messages and medical care to Palau. During the German Administration, the local people carried out governmental policies. They prohibited the sale of alcohol, controlled firearms and restricted the settlement of Europeans. By 1909, European "beachcombers" had to register and pay tax.

The Germans appointed Mr. James Gibbons as their Administration's representative. Through Gibbons, the German administration dealt directly with Chief *Ibedul,* Chief *Reklai* and "cooperative" chiefs. The Germans ignored other chiefs, regardless of their rank. Mr. James Gibbons was a Jamaican-English immigrant. He lived in Palau from the 1870's until his death in 1904. Gibbons married into Chief *Ibedul's* clan and acted as his translator. During 1902, James Gibbons became chief of police and started a police academy. Gibbons opened the first jail in Koror. Five local "policeman" enforced German rules. Before he died, Gibbons started the Seventh Day Adventist (SDA) Church. To this day, the Gibbons family remain a stronghold in the SDA Church.

In 1901, the Southwest Islands came under the German administration. In 1906, the people of the Southwest Islands relocated to Yap, Saipan and Palau because a typhoon destroyed their villages. Chief *Ibedul* designated

an area in Koror called *Ngarakebesang* for the Southwest Islanders to resettle. Spanish priests and brothers departed, leaving a Catholic community of 140 out of a population of over 4,000 people. In 1907, the German Capuchins arrived in force. In 1910, the German Capuchins built a second Catholic mission in *Melekeok*. Father Basilius cared for the parish and Brother Kleophas assisted him. Catholicism spread to *Ngarchelong, Airai* and *Aimeliik.* A typhoon struck in 1912 and demolished all the mission buildings in *Melekeok, Aimeliik, Airai* and *Ngatmel.* Only Koror's mission escaped serious damage. The Germans were allies with the Capuchins in their campaign for reform. Laws prohibited inter-village warfare, institutionalized concubinage and limited lengthy celebrations and major feasts. Chiefs had to request permission from the local administers to hold large parties and community meetings. The Germans felt these customs were a waste of time.

The German administration tried to develop a commercially viable copra industry in Palau. In 1902 they shipped a large supply of coconuts which were planted on *Babeldaob.* By 1904 there were 40,000 trees planted. German efforts to develop coconut plantations were unsuccessful due to bad weather, insect infestations and unenthusiastic local labor. Police inspected and fined landowners with diseased coconut trees. (The Berlin Museum still has Palauan money collected as fines.) The Germans began the production of phosphate in *Angaur* and copra production in Koror and *Babeldaob.* During 1909, Germany established a second administration station in *Angaur* because of the lucrative phosphate industry. In 1913 the Phosphate Stock Company had 10 Germans, 500 Palauans and 100 Chinese workers. Laborers worked 9-hour days at $4.27 a month! The South Sea Phosphate Stock Company produced the most important export and generated profitable revenues for the Germans. By 1910, Germany administered the Marianas,

Orange Beach, Peleliu Island, Palau. Scene of one of the bloodiest battles of World War II.

American assault vehicle near Bloody Nose Ridge.

17

A PERSONAL TOUR OF PALAU

CHAPTER 1: A HISTORY OF CONFLICT

Carolines, Palau and Marshall Islands under one government. Meanwhile, the Japanese established the South Seas Trading Company. The Japanese company developed fishing and copra (coconut meat) trades in Palau despite efforts by the German administration to stop them.

During 1908 to 1910, the German Südsee expedition assigned two anthropologists to Palau. Dr. Augustin Krämer studied the main archipelago of Palau. Anneliese Eilers studied the more distant Southwest Islands. Together, they documented Palauan social structure, house building, land use, art, beliefs and practices. Dr. Krämer's work includes five published volumes on Palau from 1917 to 1929. Dr. Krämer's work was the most important contribution documenting Palauan history in the 20th Century.

On August 23, 1914, Japan declared war on Germany. On October 8, 1914, World War I began. The Japanese naval task forces established a naval district in Chuuk. Shortly after the war began, two Japanese warships steamed into *Malakal* Harbor to claim Palau. In September 1914, the Japanese deported all German nationals, except their missionaries. In 1915, five Capuchins and five Franciscan sisters bid farewell to their

"All gave some, some gave all." Monument to commemorate the bravery and valor of the fighting men on both sides atop Bloody Nose Ridge.

Church community of 400 people.

The German Administration ended in Palau. From 1914 to 1920, the Japanese Imperial Navy administrated in Palau. The newly established League of Nations settled World War I disputes in 1919. Against the will of the United States, the League of Nations mandate awarded Palau to Japan. This mandate prohibited slavery and the building of military bases or structures. The mandate further promoted the well being of the Palauan people and allowed missionary work. For the first time, formal education by a foreign country was mandatory throughout Palau. Japan required all Palauans to attend school for three years.

On Easter Sunday, 1922, a typhoon struck, destroying many mission buildings. As a result, the Jesuits concentrated their missionary work in Koror.

It is important to note the effort of indigenous people to establish the *Modekngei* religion. In 1915, a handful of Palauans formed the *Modekngei* religion in northern *Babeldaob*. *Modekngei* believed in the power of the clan and village gods.

Eventually, Peleliu became the stronghold of the *Modekngei* religion. However, in 1926, a high ranking woman from Peleliu with strong community influence

converted from *Modekngei* to Catholism. She helped in an active campaign to convert 160 people within a few years. Catholicism continued to expand further south to *Angaur.* About 100 Chamorro Catholic familes working in the phosphate mines spread their faith within that community. In 1930, a priest visited *Sonsorol* for the first time since 1710. Within two years, the entire Southwest Island community, including the community in *Ngarkebesang,* was Catholic. Membership in the Catholic Church jumped from 400 to over 1000 members between 1921 to 1931. The Catholic community erected a new concrete church in Koror and dedicated it on Easter Sunday, 1935. Chief *Reklai* Tellei of *Melekeok* supported the church up to his death in 1937.

The Japanese did not impose their faith upon the Palauan people. The State religion of Japan at the time was Shintoism. Shintoists believe that the emperor of Japan was a descendant of the sun and therefore a god. In 1940, the Japanese built a Shinto shrine in Palau. At the time, the second largest in the world.

In 1922, the Japanese established a civilian South Seas Government administered by Governor Toshiro Tezuka. The Japanese Administration transformed Koror from a single main road with 42 houses and scattered palm trees to a busy metropolis. By 1930, Koror had 250 govern-ment-built houses for an immigrant population of over 2,000 people. By 1935, about 25,000 Japanese resided in Koror. Koror had stores, tree lined sidewalks, sewage and

power facilities. On *Babeldaob,* coconut plantations and pineapple farms flourished. Bauxite mining started in *Ngardmau.* By 1940, the Japanese moved most Chamorro laborers to *Ngardmau* to work the newly opened mines.

OEK building in downtown Koror. This building houses both the Senate and House of Representatives of the Palau National Congress.

The Japanese heavily exploited fisheries products. Small communities of foreign laborers began to populate areas of agricultural and fisheries production. In December 1939, the Japanese moved Palauans out of *Angaur* in order to expand their phosphate mining operations. The Japanese administration created confusion about land ownership. The Japanese bought or confiscated clan land. Clan lands became public lands. Today, Palauans are still trying to settle land ownership.

During 1935, Japan withdrew from the League of Nations and violated the non-military mandate. Palau became a closed military area with heavy fortifications. The Japanese ordered the construction of seaplane ramps and large gun placements overlooking the reef passages and harbors. In 1937, the Japanese closed Peleliu to all foreigners. The Japanese prepared for war and forced the people of Peleliu to resettle in *Babeldaob.* Chief *Obak* of Peleliu arranged for the relocation of his people with

Chief *Madrengebuked* of *Ngaraard*. Chief *Obak* knew that *Ngaraard* had extensive taro patches that could feed his people in times of hardship. Chief *Madrengebuked* took in many families himself and arranged sponsors for each Peleliu family. To this day, there is a strong bond between the people of *Ngaraard* and Peleliu.

Chief *Ibedul*, Yutaka B. Gibbons, Paramount Chief of Koror.

On the morning of December 7, 1941, "a date which will live in infamy," the Japanese attacked Pearl Harbor. World War II began in the Pacific. During 1944, the Japanese laboriously dug intricate cave systems in Peleliu and *Angaur* and fortified for war. In the spring and summer of 1944, Americans began bombing Japanese ships and facilities in Palau. In July, the Japanese evacuated three Jesuit priests from their mission and confined them in temporary barracks. Later, the Japanese sent the priests to *Ngatpang* where they eventually disappeared. Palauans believe the Japanese executed the priests in late September. On September 15, 1944, the invasion of Peleliu and *Angaur* began with amphibious assaults by the U.S. Marines. The purpose of the Palau invasion was to protect General MacArthur's flank for the upcoming invasion of the Philippines.

The thick forest canopy disguised the treacherous limestone cliffs and intricate cave systems designed and fortified by the Japanese. After three months of bloody battles, the Americans defeated the Japanese. The war claimed the lives of over 1,800 American and more than 10,000 Japanese soldiers. Five hundred Palauans died (10% of the population) during World War II. As the battle ended, General Nakagawa and Major General Muria committed suicide in the traditional Japanese manner.

World War II was everybody's battle. All gave some and some gave all. No other war in history affected so many

families worldwide. It is hard to imagine how the people of Peleliu and *Angaur* felt upon their return. The battles totally destroyed their islands and left behind many dangerous explosives. The generation that experienced this war is slowly disappearing. My mother-in-law, Ngemelas Kitalong, now 83 years old, still recalls the fear, hunger and death of WWII. Her family hid in caves and scavenged for food. Her sister Ebau Oiterong recalls trying to feed her hungry children. Her breasts had no milk. Men did not fish on the reefs because they feared the Japanese would shoot them on sight. Ngemelas's young children died, unable to receive any medical treatment. She saw bodies of men blown apart. She has many unforgettable and painful memories of war. Yet Ngemelas and many in her age group have many good memories of the Japanese before the war. Palauans shared their food with starving Japanese soldiers.

Japanese ships still lie on the bottom of the lagoon. Palauans continue to find pieces of plane wreckage scattered on the forest floor and lagoon bottom. At high vantage points you can see exposed pillboxes where soldiers hid. Remnants of military fortifications remain where cannons once stood. Cement watch posts line the limestone ridges. Old unexploded bombs, mines and bullets lie hidden in the bush. Ordinance teams screen the land and sea before every major earth-moving project. Today, American and Japanese memorials commemorate the soldiers in *Angaur*, Peleliu, Koror and *Babeldaob*. Sunken ships and planes now attract tourists worldwide...remnants of war that bring battles to life once more.

My first visit to Peleliu was during the summer of 1977. For the first time in my life, World War II became real to me. Alone, I walked for hours along the hot limestone roads. I thought of my father and the rare times he told his story of the war. My father, at the age of 18, entered the U.S. Army. Dad was the son of German immigrants to the United States. He fought battles in the

Philippines and Papau New Guinea. He watched many comrades die. Hundreds of men, loaded down with gear, drowned, just trying to get off the boats. During my youth, I never once saw my father swim. He escaped death five times during the war. He contracted tropical infections. Medical officers hospitalized him in the Philippines. He said he never killed a man directly, but knew men died with grenades he threw into the caves. He has no desire ever to come back to this region of the world. He has too many painful memories.

When I reached the beaches of Peleliu, I saw large scraps of rusted metal from ships scattered on the shore…ships of war that carried hundreds of men to their deaths. The weathering by rain and ocean waves had formed a treacherous shoreline of jagged limestone with razor sharp projections and hidden crevices. There was an eeriness about the beaches during mid-afternoon. I felt it more when walking alone on these beaches. There was a looming presence of war. I imagined soldiers, fighting to reach the shore. Powerful waves crashing on each young man with guns shooting from all directions. I imagined a beautiful blue lagoon slowly turning red.

In September 1994, Palau commemorated the fiftieth anniversary of World War II. The celebration began in the center of the main village of Peleliu. U.S. Military groups marched onto the field in full uniform with a full band playing. Palauan men and women marched in colorful muumuus and hats. The crowds were cheering and clapping. Then, I vividly remember the last group that marched onto the field. A small band of older Japanese men marched onto the field, carrying the Japanese flag. The loud cheers turned to quiet whispers as the crowd watched the elderly Japanese march onto the field. Then I had a flashback of a visit to the Pearl Harbor Memorial, where I overheard American tourists whisper about the few Asians present. I recalled my visit to the Hiroshima Memorial in 1978. At the Memorial, myself and Nancy were the only Americans witnessing, through

photographs, the agony the Japanese people endured from the atomic bomb. I realize that there are many innocent victims on both sides of war.

Once the speeches and parade were over, we went to visit the battlegrounds of Peleliu.

Chief Reklai, Raphael B. Ngirmang, Paramount Chief of Melekeok State.

The Palauans gave well-planned tours and plenty of bottled water was available on the buses. The Palauan hosts worried about the veterans. The now elderly men were unaccustomed to the heat and humidity. The Palauans especially worried about the veteran's climb up the steep steps of Bloody Nose Ridge. This Ridge in the *Umurbrogal* Mountains is the site of the worst battle of Peleliu. The elderly veterans were real troopers once again. Up the steep steps they all climbed with their wives, children and grandchildren. The determined veterans wanted to show their families where they fought so long ago.

I wanted to be with the veterans that day. I thought that somehow, by being with them, I could better understand what my father and many men had experienced during WWII. As our bus went through the now thick jungles of secondary forests, the veterans stared out the windows. One veteran said, "I didn't know where I was then and I don't know where I am now." As we approached each battlefield I saw different reactions from the men. Some had excitement in their eyes as they explained to their families how they got up the beach. Many were silent. I did not see tears. There was only silence. One veteran traveled in his original fatigues, decorated with war metals. He carried his gun as well. Television crews and camera operators put the spotlight on him. He, unlike many, did not want to forget that he fought in Peleliu.

The Philippines became my family's battleground once more during June of 1996, twenty years after I first

walked Peleliu's shores. I contracted a deadly strain of the bacteria leptospirosis. My family evacuated me to St. Luke's Hospital in the Philippines. My family in Palau came with me. My brother, sister and mother flew in from the United States to be with me. After a few weeks, my condition miraculously improved. The doctors said I am very lucky to be alive today. While I recuperated, my mother decided to fulfill my father's wish. Dad wanted mom to visit the memorial dedicated to the 55,000 soldiers who died in the Pacific during WWII. So, mom with her daughter, son and two grandsons saw her husband's battle-ground for the first time. She saw thousands upon thousands of white crosses. Her eyes filled with tears.

In 1947, Palau and the Micronesia districts became part of the United States Trust Territory of the Pacific Islands. The United Nations mandated this Trust that the United States administrated. From 1948 to 1951, the United States Department of the Navy administrated in Palau. During 1952, the Department of Interior began administrating in the Trust Territory. Americans based their central office in Hawaii, then Guam and later Saipan. Their goal was to make the Micronesian Islands self-governing and independent. During this time the first American schools opened in Palau. Palauans received their first college degrees. President John Kennedy established the Peace Corps. The Peace Corps volunteers consisted of college graduates and working professionals whom came to train and teach. The volunteers taught specific trades upon the request of the local governments. The first Peace Corps came to Palau in the 1965. I came to Palau as a Peace Corps volunteer in 1977. The only branch of the U.S. military present in Palau was the Civic Action Team or the Seabees. The Seabees still help with community projects.

In 1975, an American businessman, Robert Panero

President Kuniwo Nakamura signs
Declaration of Independence, October 1, 1994.

selected Palau's northern reef passage, *Kossol* Passage as the proposed site for a superport. He wanted to develop a port to transship and store 500,000 tons of crude oil for supertankers from the Persian Gulf in transit to Japan and the U.S. The superport was a 5 billion-dollar project. Chief *Ibedul* of Koror, Yutaka Gibbons with the help of Mr. Moses Uludong and many concerned Palauans formed the "Save Palau" organization. The "Save Palau" organization fought against this environmentally unsound proposal and won.

In 1978, the Marshall Islands, Palau, Kosrae, Yap, Chuuk and Pohnpei voted on a proposed Constitution of the Federated States of Micronesia. Palau rejected the Micronesian Constitution under the initiative of Roman Tmetuchl. On July 9, 1980, Palau adopted its own constitution while still under the U.S. Trusteeship. Palau's political system is similar to the United States democratic government. The Congress of Palau is the *Olbiil Era Kelulau* (OEK) or "House of Whispers." The traditional council of chiefs act as advisories to the Executive Branch. From 1947 to 1980, Koror was the district center of the U.S. Trusteeship of Palau and then became the provisional capital of the Republic of Palau.

In 1980, Palauans elected the First President of the Republic of Palau, Mr. Haruo Remeliik. General strikes occurred during 1981 and 1982 because of unrest among the Palauan community. Local police killed one striker

Heads of State of Pacific Nations attending the 30th South Pacific Forum
(now called Secretariat of Pacific Communities) in Palau, October 1999.

and wounded several others. Palauans firebombed President Remeliik's office. Palauans called upon Chief *Ibedul* to intervene. President Remeliik contracted IPESCO, International Power System Ltd., a British power company, to build a 16-megawatt power plant in *Aimeliik*. President Remeliik depended on Compact of Free Association funds to finance the power plant.

In 1983, Palauans held the first popular vote to ratify Palau's Compact of Free Association (COFA) with the United States. The COFA provided a payment of $517 million to Palau over a 15-year period. In return, the U.S. had land use rights for military bases and the right to operate nuclear warships in Palau's territorial waters. The Palau Superior Court nullified the first plebiscite because the Palauan Constitution mandates a 75% majority vote for ratification. Palau held a second plebiscite on September 4, 1983, resulting in a 66% majority vote but not the constitutionally mandated 75%. In January 1985 Palauans reelected President Remeliik for a second term. In April 1985 Palau defaulted on a $32 million dollar

loan for the IPSECO power plant. On the night of June 30, 1985, assassins murdered President Remeliik outside his home. Vice President Alfonso Oiterong became the second President of the Republic of Palau. By December 1985, the banks sued Palau for $35 million. President Oiterong called for a special presidential election in August 1985. On October 25, 1985, Mr. Lazarus Salii was sworn in as the third President of the Republic of Palau.

Palau and the United States renegotiated and amended the Compact of Free Association (COFA). The amended COFA stated that the United States agrees not to "use, test, store or dispose of nuclear, toxic chemical gas or biological weapons intended for use in warfare," under Article II, Section 321(c). A small island nation stood its ground for a nuclear-free zone against the world's most powerful nation. In February 1986, a third plebiscite to ratify the amended Compact of Free Association (COFA) resulted in a 72% majority vote but was still below the constitutionally mandated 75%. In December 1986 a

fourth plebiscite produced a 66% majority vote. The Palau government money ran out, so the administration cut salaries and working hours. Government furloughs created unrest and Palauans demonstrated.

On June 30, 1987 the fifth plebiscite to ratify the Compact of Free Association (COFA) obtained a 68% majority vote but not the constitutionally mandated 75%. In August 1987, by public law, the people of Palau amended two sections of their constitution relating to the nuclear issues. The sixth plebiscite to ratify the COFA received 73% of the vote. President Salii declared that the Compact of Free Association passed ratification. Anti-compact leaders, Chief *Ibedul* and Roman Bedor, sued the government, but later dropped their lawsuit. A group of female leaders reinstated the lawsuit on the grounds of the constitutionally mandated 75%. On Labor Day, a sudden power failure occurred at night. Adversaries firebombed the house of one of these women. That same night, assassins shot and killed Roman Bedor's father outside his son's office. Men fired shots at the house of Senate Speaker, Santos Olikong. Shocked by the violence, the United States Department of Interior delayed ratification of the Compact in 1988. There were rumors about payoffs to leaders during the IPSECO negotiations. On August 20, 1988, President Salii died at his home. Vice President Thomas Remengesau became the fourth President of the Republic of Palau until the November election of 1988.

In 1989, Mr. Ngiratkel Etpison became the fifth President of the Republic of Palau. President Etpison's administration was economically and politically stable. On February 6, 1990, Palauans held the seventh plebiscite on the amended Compact of Free Association (COFA) with the lowest approval of all (60.5% of the vote). In April 1992, over 3,000 pro-COFA citizens, with the active support of President Etpison, submitted an initiative to the Palauan Congress. The pro-COFA citizens requested Congress to hold a Constitutional referendum to amend the required 75% vote to a simple majority to ratify COFA. Congress agreed to hold a Constitutional referendum if Palau and the United Stated agreed to 2 conditions: 1) reduce the terms of the COFA from 50 to 15 years and 2) reduce the size of Palauan

President Tommy E. Remengesau, Jr. takes the oath of office administered by Chief Justice Arthur Ngiraklsong as his father, former President Thomas Remengesau, Sr., and the First Lady, Debbie Remengesau, look on.

Vice President Sandra Sumang Pierantozzi, the first female Vice President of Palau is sworn in by Supreme Court Associate Justice Kate Salii, Palau's first female Supreme Court Justice. Honorary Consular Correspondent to Italy and spouse to the Vice President, Marcello Pierantozzi, looks on.

lands used for U.S. Military purposes. The Palauans voted to approve the referendum on November 4, 1992. The Supreme Court accepted the results of the referendum. The newly amended Palau Constitution lowered the COFA approval from 75% to that of a simple majority (50% + 1) vote. In the November 4, 1992 election, the people chose their sixth President, Mr. Kuniwo Nakamura and their fourth National Congress. On November 9, 1993, a decade of intense legal and political conflict came to a close. The eighth plebiscite ratified the Compact of Free Association with the United States with a 64% majority vote.

After a century of foreign domination, Palau achieved independence as a sovereign nation in free association with the United States. The Palauans chose to amend their Constitution by suspending the anti-nuclear provision. The simple majority voted to free Palau of the Trusteeship system. Palau is the 185th member of the United Nations. "My country will be one of the smallest members of this

President Tommy Remengesau, Jr.

august body, but we are large in things that count," President Kuniwo Nakamura told the United Nations. The road to independence was a difficult one, marked with political conflict, violence, assassinations and legal challenges. The U.S. has military land-use rights and authority over Palau's defense. The fifteenth anniversary of the Compact will be October 1, 2009. At that time, the United States financial assistance will cease. The United States disbursed most of the money during the first five years of the Compact. Palau's challenge is to become economically sustainable by October 1, 2009.

The last traditional war in Palau occurred over a hundred years ago. Yet, elders still teach young men leadership strategies, personal discipline and the way of politics. Palauans make alliances with each other. Palauans skilled in the art of persuasion and intrigue continue to lead the direction of fellow Palauans and foreigners. Elders punish and then forget the crimes, as in the past. It is a complex game. The Executive Branch together with the OEK (*Olbiil Era Kelulau*) take center stage. The traditional leaders, the Executive Branch, the Senate, the House of Delegates and Palauan community work together to mold the future of the Republic.

The National Congress, *Olbiil Era Kelulau* (OEK) adopted several master plans to guide the Republic into the 21st century. As we take our first steps into this new century, Palau continues to progress. A new capitol city in *Melekeok* is being constructed. A 53-mile road in *Babeldaob* is in progress. A new suspension bridge is replacing the old KB Bridge. Our debt to IPESCO power plant is paid. The air is full of issues and questions about the future of Palau.

Palau's newly elected President, Tommy Esang Remengesau, Jr., whose campaign slogan to "preserve the best and improve the rest" demonstrates his grassroots approach to leadership. President Remengesau Jr. together with Vice President Sandra Sumang Pierantozzi, the *Olbiil Era Kelulau* and traditional leaders now steer the course of Palau's future.

REFERENCES

Bowden -Kerby, A. 1984. Unpublished class notes on the Geology of Palau.

A History of Palau. 1976. *Volume 1. Traditional Palau: The First Europeans*, Palau Community Action Agency.

A History of Palau. 1977. *Volume 2. Traders and Whalers Spanish Administration German Administration.* Palau Community Action Agency.

Tia Belau Newspaper, Special Issue, *1st Anniversary of Compact.* Editor Moses Uludong.

Micronesia's Yesterday. 1973. Editor James Vincent. Trust Territory Printing Office, Saipan.

Military Geology of Palau Islands, Caroline Islands. 1956. Chief of Engineers, U.S. Army.

A Collection of Palauan Legends. Unpublished.

Hezel, F. X. 1991. *The Catholic Church in Micronesia.* Loyola University Press Chicago.

Trust Territory of the Pacific Islands. *1993 Annual Report.*

4th Micronesian Games. August 1-9, 1998. *Souvenir Program. 1998.*

Rechebei Diaz Elizabeth and Samuel F. Mc Phetres. 1997. *History of Palau.* Bureau of Curriculum and Instruction. Ministry of Education. Republic of Palau.

Trust Territory of the Pacific Islands. 1990. *43rd Annual Report to the United Nations on the Administration of the Trust Territory of the Pacific Islands.*

25

Fishing the Reef and Lagoons

Fishing fills a man's soul. Ask any Palauan man what he would rather do more than anything else and it will be fishing for sure. If they miss a week they can survive. If two weeks, oh boy! If a month, they must be sick. The fisherman observes the moon and tides for the right day and time. The day before, he and his fishing companions plan the trip. He mends nets, sharpens spears, checks the rubber on spearguns and the platoon's line. The spark plugs are cleaned and a few spares are purchased. New batteries are put in the flashlight. The outboard motor's filter is checked to make sure no water is inside. If there is, the filter is cleaned. The gas tanks are well rinsed before new fuel is added. The ropes, anchor and fishing gear are set in their proper place. The boat is set. The most important supplies: betel nut *(buuch)*, leaves *(kebui)* and lime *(chaus)* are added to his basket. In the early morning, his wife prepares a lunch of fried fish, taro, a hot thermos of coffee, sweet rolls and a jug of drinking water.

You have not been fishing? Oh, what you have been missing! There are many ways to fish in Palau. You can fish by gleaning the reefs, throwing spears, handlining, shoot-ing with spearguns, casting nets, setting nets, trolling, casting with rod and reel, harpooning and setting traps. Let's take a look at some of these techniques and see if you would like to try something new this weekend…

Gleaning the reefs at night with your lantern is fun for all the family. For a few days during certain months, the fringing reefs have very low tides at night. Everyone finds a flashlight or lantern and heads out to the reefs by midnight. Women drag their metal basins *(tarai)* containing their small woven baskets with personal belongings *(tet)* and small knives. They scan the reefs with their lights. At night, sea cucumbers like *Actinopyga miliaris (cheremrum)* emerge out of the sands. The rabbitfish, *Signaus fuscescens (meas)* move slowly and sleep between the blades of seagrass. Tiger cowries, *Cypraena tiger (buich)* crawl along the sand. The blue reef crab, *Portunus pelagicus (kmai)* hide between grass and coral. Groups of women collect marine organisms as they walk. A few women use small hand spears to spear the sleeping rabbitfish. Men fish with spearguns and use floating foam containers (platoons) to hold their catch in deeper waters. In the past, there was

Photo at right: Use of sporting goods store fishing rod and reel is a fairly recent innovation in Palau.

a greater abundance of larger sized fish and marine organisms. It was easy to catch and collect a full load in a short time. Yet, the community still enjoys these reef activities with family and friends. Groups slowly scatter as you watch the lights spread out over the reefs throughout the early dark morning hours. You can look out and see 50 lights along the reef. As the tide waters rise, the lights combine into a few small clusters and head to the shore.

Old man mends his nets at the dock at *Ngeremelengui.*

Young boys still hurry home from school to fish. They fix their three pronged spears days before. They cut a thin bamboo-like tree, *Schizostachyum lima (lild)* and take it to their uncle's house. Their uncle shows them how to take

make a chase as they lightly race over the reef and throw their spears. This method is called *"oltoir."* Another method of catching fish on the reef is through the use of a stationary net called a *kesokes* net. When a *kesokes* net is full of fish, the community helps in the harvest. The boys then practice their spear throwing skills on the trapped fish. If there is no net to trap them, they must chase the fish into a shallow spot themselves. While practicing, the boys learn how the fish move along the reef and their way of escape. They learn which fish are fast and which are slow. My husband, Clarence was raised by his grandmother. He would wait until he saw an uncle leave to fish and ask to go along. He had no father to take him. Many uncles and older cousins patiently brought him along to learn. Now, he too, takes along young boys with him. They are so eager and try so hard to catch their first fish.

Handlines are used during the day but are more common at night. Groups of women and men fish together. Families, couples or friends go out just before sunset. The basic skills of setting lines and tying weights and hooks are learned during your youth. The true skill is in catching the fish. Once you throw your

Three prong spear head attached to 7-ft. bamboo stick makes an excellent spear for shallow water fishing.

apart a twisted cable wire to make three metal prongs. They find thin copper wire to tightly wind around the *"lild"* to hold their prongs in place. After a quick snack, they grab their spears and run to the reef before the tide gets too high. Then off on their rafts or on foot they go to find their fish. They watch the ripples on the surface and

line, the lead weight sinks below the surface. The line becomes slack when it has reached the bottom. If there is a swift current, the line drifts and never touches the bottom. You can add more weight to bring the line downward. Your fingers tell you if it is a large or small fish nibbling. Once you sense that the bait is in the fish's

Traditional Palauan fishing gear made up of monofiliment line wrapped around a piece of aged bamboo. Palauans can cast the hook and bait with amazing accuracy.

Larger sized hooks are for larger sized fish in similar families and more. Handlining for coral trout in the spring and for groupers in the summer makes for an exciting time. *Ulong* Channel, *Denges* Pass, *Ngeremlengui* Pass and others are aggregation sites for groupers. In the past, the fish markets were overloaded with grouper and their freezers could not hold all the fish that were brought to them. The markets cut their prices and fishermen stopped bringing them in. Today, Palauan law restricts fishing at grouper aggregation sites during breeding season in the spring and summer months.

During the spring of 1997, while passing through *Airai* bay, I saw families fishing. Two young boys were huddled on their raft preparing their lines. Together they stood up, swung their arms over head and cast their lines into the water. Their raft was in shallow water on the reef. As we turned the bend, their father was just putting on his mask and descending into the water with his gun to spear fish along the deep water of the lagoon. Their father towed his sons' bamboo raft behind his boat and left his sons to line fish in a safe place. Nearby, a husband and wife were in their canoe casting their lines over the shallow reef. Casting your line over your head with a light line and hook (less than size no.5) with an optional light weight is called *"mengereel."* The bait is usually the intestines of the sea cucumber, *Stichopus variegatus (ngimes).* The catch consists of yellow-lip

mouth, you must quickly yank the line to snag the fish. If you are too slow, the fish will just nibble away at your bait. A very large fish can break your line. Women can be very adept at handlining and are good competitors for their male partners. Often, when a line is thrown, a small chant is called out to the fish below calling them to come and eat.

Handlining involves one to three men using as many as four lines with three hooks on each line. A weight is placed at the bottom of the line to hold it down in the water. The best seat on the boat varies. There is always one lucky person or seat. The best bait is the small herring, *Herklotsichthys quadrimaculatus (mekebud),* when freshly caught. If it gets mushy, it is better to use squid *(luut)* because it stays on the hook better. You put the hook through the eyes of two herrings and then again through the body of the fish. The best hook is number 4 and 5 to catch snappers *(Lutjanids),* emperors *(Lethrinids)* and groupers *(Serranids).*

Palauan raft called a *"brer."*
There are many of these in existence today.

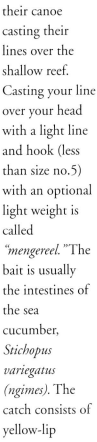

Women and kids fish the reefs for supper.

caused a population decrease over the past twenty years. The juvenile humphead wrass *(ngimer)* is a common catch while handlining. *"Ngimer"* may look like a mature reef fish, but it is not. It needs years to grow and reproduce. If you catch a juvenile wrass *(ngimer)*, it is best to let it go.

Spearfishing is the most common method of fishing in Palau. Night spearfishing is especially popular. Fish targeted are surgeonfish *(Acanthurids)*, emperors *(Lethrinids)*, jacks *(Carangids)*, sweetlips *(Plectorhinchus* spp.*)*, groupers *(Epinephelus* spp. and *Plectropomus* spp.*)*, rabbitfish *(Siganids)*, snappers *(Lutjanids)* and parrotfish *(Scarids)*. A wide variety of fish are speared at night. Some fishermen can catch 400 pounds of fish in a single night! The largest parrotfish, the humphead parrotfish *Bolbometopon muricatum (kemedukl)* has become a victim of night spearfishing. Some fishermen know their sleeping

emperor, *Lethrinus obsoletus (chudech)*, the small grouper, *Epinephelus merra (chemirchorech)* and the bream fish, *Pentapodus caninus (chibars)*. If you use a heavier line and add a small weight just above the larger hooks (size no.6-8) and throw the line outward over a shallow reef, it is called *"omdesakl."* You catch larger fish like yellowlip emperor, *Lethrinus xanthochilus (mechur)*, the long nose emperor, *Lethrinus elongatus (melangmud)*, the large red snapper, *Lutjanus bohar (kedesau)* and the humpback snapper, *Lutjanus gibbus (keremlal)*.

A very special fish is the large humphead wrasse, *Cheilinus undulatus (maml)*. *"Maml"* is a highly prized fish and a treat for chiefs during customs. The *"maml"* takes years to grow and reproduce. Overfishing has

Young boys spearfishing on the shallow reef flats of Koror.

grounds well, making them easy targets as they sleep. At one time there were thousands of *"kemedukl"* that slept on the fringing reefs. Now you are lucky to see a dozen together at any given time or place. The adult humphead parrotfish has tasty meat and it is a good show-fish at a buffet. Net fishermen in northern *Babeldaob* are also

targeting the juvenile humphead parrotfish *(berdebed).* Palauan law protects juvenile humphead parrotfish because they take many years to mature.

Night spearfishing involves at least two men on the boat. One man may stay on the boat and maneuver the boat while two or three go into the water with flashlights. If the fishing is good in one area they may stay for forty-five minutes or more. However, they usually move to several different spots during the night. Once in the water, they spread out in different directions with their flashlights. They spear at close range using small spearguns that require less power to cock. The rabbitfish, *Siganus fuscescens (meas)* in *Airai* bay are easy targets at night. Your face is within inches of the fish. If not for their stinging dorsal spines, you could easily just grab them with your hands. I was painfully stung twice while cleaning rabbitfish. To me this fish is more dangerous dead than alive!

Daytime spearfishing is more challenging than nighttime spearing. A fisherman is a hunter. He stalks a fish, follows its movements and waits for the right moment to spear. The

Melekeok boy tears strips of octopus tentacle for bait.

daytime speargun is long and powerful with a spear attached to the gun by line and propelled by a tautly pulled rubber hose. Fish are more active during the day and must be speared from a distance. A fisherman must have good aim. Rabbitfish, parrotfish, surgeonfish, snappers, sweetlips and groupers are caught during the day. The best spear fishermen can spear open ocean fish that are usually caught while trolling. I watched as my husband, Clarence tackled a large king mackerel fish *Scomberomorus commerson (ngelngal)* weighing about twenty pounds. He called me to bring the boat to him. The fish was circling him and pulling at his gun. Clarence had to dive underwater several times while maintaining a tight grip on his gun. His gun was attached to his spear by a taut line. The king mackerel struggled frantically trying to free itself. Finally he got the mackerel by the gills, pulled out the spear from its head and threw it into the boat. I kept my distance as it thrashed from side to side with its mouth full of sharp teeth.

Cast nets *(bidekill)* are small circular nets with light weights around the edge. It is held over the shoulder with one hand holding the edge ready to throw it over a school of passing fish. Cast nets are used to catch the small herring, *Herklotsichthys quadrimaculatus (mekebud),* a popular baitfish used for line fishing. Small flocks of black noddy, *Anous minutus (bedaoch)* pursue

A nice catch by any standard.

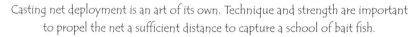

A common site in Palau. Spear guns can reach 7 ft. in length and do not easily fit inside the car. No doubt about it though, the boys are going fishing.

herring schools that look like a dark cloud moving in the water. Herring are found near inner coves, semi-enclosed lakes and along the beach edge in the shade of over hanging trees. During the early morning at *Ulong* Island, several boats come by to catch herring along the beach. They are getting bait for fishing.

Fishermen may cast their nets from the boat or from the shore. They must jump in to retrieve it. In the spring, cast nets are used to catch rabbitfish, *Siganus fuscescens (meas)* as they go past certain areas along the fringing reefs.

Set nets or "*kesokes*" nets require people working to-gether. One man can do it but it is very difficult and laborious. The *kesokes* net is set in a "V" shape

formation. During the day, the pocket at the end of the "V" is placed in the deepest water. Stakes made from the young mangrove tree, *Rhizophora mucronata (tebechel)* are used to hold the *kesokes* net in place. The ends are sharpened and stuck into the sand. The nets are weighted along the bottom with lead and have a mesh size of two and one half inches. Some nets are over 100 feet long. Set nets can catch more fish in a single day than any other fishing method. During the daylight hours of April through September, *kesokes* nets are set during the last hours of a falling tide.

Fishermen leave a small gap at the apex of this v-shaped net and place a pocket shaped net between the two long ends of the stretched net. Mangrove branches with leaves are placed in this deeper pocket net because fish seek refuge among the leaves. As the tide goes out, the fish are funneled toward this pocket and are eventually trapped as the reef becomes exposed. During October to March, *kesokes* nets are set at night during the last hours of falling

Casting net deployment is an art of its own. Technique and strength are important to propel the net a sufficient distance to capture a school of bait fish.

CHAPTER 2: FISHING THE REEF AND LAGOONS

tides. A pocket is unnecessary during the night, because fish do not move towards the deeper water, but just sleep where the net blocks their movement.

Experienced fishermen know where fish will enter and leave the seagrass beds during the outgoing tides. They know the areas where there are few rocks or coral that would snag the net or

Before nylon nets were available, fish traps were built of coral rocks. Fish would school in the point of the arrow. At low tide, fish were caught by spear or crude nets fashioned from plam leaves.

leave a gap for the fish to escape. If they plan to set a net at night, the apex of the "V" shaped net is marked with a stick and reference points on land are noted. These reference points are used to help set the net at night because it is hard to see. (If fishermen set their nets during the daylight hours, they do not need to mark the place for the apex of the net because they can see it.) Once the apex is marked, the fishermen let out sections of net on either side. The 50-feet sections of the

net are tied to the mangrove stakes, top and bottom. Additional sections are added as needed. The mangrove stakes are set about twenty to twenty-five feet apart. These stakes act like a brace to hold the net upright during changes in tidal currents. If the currents are stronger than usual, the stacks are spaced closer together. The apex of the net is placed just beyond the point where the reef will be exposed at low tide. It is a slightly deeper area that remains covered with water. During

Bottom fishing using a dugout canoe is a fading tradition though still occasionally seen.

Modern, brightly colored lures are used in trolling nowadays replacing the hand-made lures of chicken feathers and flowers.

lily plant, *Hymenocallis littoralis (bischrad)* were used as lures before commercial ones were available. Heavier lines (50-pounds or greater) are either tied off to the back cleats of the boat or attached to fishing rods. Men may sit on either side holding the lines. Trolling fisherman may use gloves and a spear. When a fish strikes, the driver slows down and the fish is pulled into the boat. As the line is pulled in, it coils by the fisherman's feet. The fish are either brought in by bare hands or with a gaff. A spear may be used to kill the fish. Trolling fish include king mackerel, *Scomberomorus commerson (ngelngal)*, wahoo, *Acanthocybium solandri (keskas)*, small barracuda, *Sphyraena genie (lolou)*, large barracuda, *Sphyraena barracuda (chai)*, the giant trevally, *Caranx ignobilis*

Barracuda are a favored catch.

the day, fish are drawn to this deeper area and trapped.

Several families used large *kesokes* nets to fish for a living. The Otei family had a three-man operation. They caught striped mackerel, *Rastrelliger kanagurta (smach)* and scad, *Selar crumenophthalmus (terekrik)*. The Eberdong family had an eight to ten man operation. They caught the forktail rabbitfish, *Siganus argenteus (beduut)*, the blue spine unicorn fish, *Naso unicornis (chum)* and the long nose emperor, *Lethrinus elongatus (melangmud)*. In 1999, the Eberdong family had a larger mesh net and set it further off shore. The Olewachel family had a two-man operation. Their catch was mainly scad, *Selar crumenophthalmus (terekrik)*. The skills required to set nets properly are passed from one generation to the next, as are other fishing methods. I now see the grandchildren of these fishing families carrying on the family fishing trade. Several net fishermen no longer use set nets. They say it is harder to catch fish and labor intensive. A sweep net made of coconut and other palm leaves *(ruul)* was used before nylon nets became common. The last sweep net was used in northern *Babeldaob* in the early 1990's. When the tide is not very low, palm leaves *(demailei)* are still used to help direct fish into the net.

Trolling is a one or two man operation, using heavy lines with lures or bait. Chicken feathers and the spider

(cheropk), bluefin trevally, *Caranx melampygus, (oruidel)*, rainbow runner, *Elagatis bipinnulatus (desui)*, mahi mahi, *Coryphaena hippurus (chersuuch)*, and sharks *(chedeng)*. Sharks are usually thrown back in the water.

Foreign long line fishing boats must be licensed to fish in Palauan waters. Their catch of tuna is usually air freighted to Japan and sold in the auction for sashimi.

quickly. We caught trevallies and jacks, barracuda and wahoo. This was my first experience and best memory of trolling.

The biggest surprise I had while trolling occurred in the fall of 1997. My friends and I were trolling the east side of Koror when we sighted large sperm whales, *Physeter catadon (medob)* in the distance. We got within a hundred feet of them. One spouted up a smelly vaporous spray of saltwater. The whales floated lazily on the surface, undisturbed by our presence. My friend Margie Falanruw jumped in the water to find out if she could hear their sounds. My friend Audrey photographed the whales, capturing a part of the excitement we felt that day.

In 1977, my friends and I were on our way to *Kayangel,* traveling on a slow wooden boat called a *"bilas"* that was powered by a small Yanmar diesel engine. The speed of the *"bilas"* was good for setting trolling lines at the back of the boat. Bena Sakuma prepared two trolling lines and baited them with freshly cut skipjack. Once he showed us how to hold the line, we each took turns holding the lines wrapped around a piece of bamboo. We caught many fish while telling stories during the four-hour trip to *Kayangel.* The time passed

Castfishing has become very popular in recent years. Casters head straight for the barrier reefs, driving their boats through the lagoon and then slow down as they approach the land side of the barrier reef. About midway,

A few of the fish caught at a recent fishing derby.

just behind the wave break, by scattered coral heads and open sandy spots, they throw their lines. Casting a good lure towards an open sandy spot and reeling it in at just the right speed will land you an assortment of fish. Groupers are a common catch, especially the small honeycomb grouper, *Epinephelus merra (chemirchorech)*, the peacock grouper, *Cephalopholis argus (mengardechelucheb)* and the saddleback grouper, *Plectropomus laevis (katuu el tiau)*. A hooked grouper heads straight to the nearest coral and hides underneath it. You may have to jump in and reach your arm into a coral hole at the risk of a few scratches. A shark may challenge your domain. It is best to let the shark have first choice. Once I was at *Airai's* barrier reef, I jumped in to get a hook that was caught on the reef. As I approached, I saw the line wrapped around a coral. The line was taut around the coral, but slack just beyond it. Then I saw a small grouper, *Epinephelus merra (chemirchorech)* sitting atop a coral head with a hooked mouth. I thought, if we had kept pulling the line, it would have snapped on the coral head and the honeycomb grouper would have gone free with the hook and some line trailing behind.

Fish caught while casting include humphead red snapper, *Lutjanus gibbus (keremlal)*, *Lutjanus semicinctus (mengelbad),* emperors, goatfish and small triggerfish. You are lucky if you get a fighting bluefin trevally, *Caranx melampygus (oruidel)* or a rainbow runner, *Elagatis bipinnulatus (desui)* on the line. In the spring, mahi mahi, *Coryphaena hippurus (chersuuch)* are abundant inside the

Palauan staples. Smoked fish, taro and tapioca. Delicious!

lagoon. These fish challenge you to keep them on the line and get them into the boat. Lines are broken and lures are taken by large fish with sharp teeth and a powerful bite. That is the price of casting. Agile casters land their fish without a scratch from the flying lines and hooks.

You can locate and cast for fish by watching the ocean birds. Dozens of birds, especially the black noddy, *Anous minutus (bedaoch)* congregate above the water surface where skipjack tuna, *Katsuwonis pelamis (katsuo)* feed. The birds feed on the same small baitfish as the skipjack tuna. You can head straight toward the birds and cast into the school of fish. Once we spotted a flock of birds just outside *Ngeremlengui's* channel. About four boats were in the vicinity. It was like an exhilarating rodeo round-up. The boats took turns circled the skipjacks while casting into the school. Even the least experienced caster among us was landing skipjacks that day! Schools of skipjacks and birds are found throughout Palau. The *Toachel Mid* Channel by the KB bridge is easily accessible by boat. One time our family went out to fish and within five minutes, Christopher, our son, caught a skipjack. We just turned back because that was all we needed for dinner. In early spring, schools of large yellowfin tuna, *Thunnus albacares (tekuu)* and skipjack come in close to the reefs near *Ngiwal*. Knowledgeable fisherman can land a hundred pounds of fish in less than an hour's time!

Skilled fishermen use harpoons to hunt. The harpoons are heavy and require strength and speed. Turtles are chased down by boat and harpooned. Another way to

Fishing stories and knowledge are often dispensed between young and old at the waters edge.

catch a turtle is to chase it down and quickly jump from the boat and catch it. Boastful fishermen tell tales of catching six to seven turtles this way.

It is interesting to note the difference in the relationship between young and elderly Palauan men when on land and on the sea. On land, the older men, called "*rubak*," are treated with respect and courtesy due to their advanced age, leadership, wealth of knowledge and position in the village. The "*rubaks*" teach through demonstration of their craft or imparting information to the willing ears of those interested. Their collective intelligence is the accumulation of years of experience and is a directive force that helps determine the course of every day village life. Once on the water, however, the younger men's contribution of strength and vitality are rewarded with tolerance and equality that arises out of partnership and mutual dependence. Young men are given temporary license to treat leaders as their peers even

to the extent of teasing them and being mildly disrespectful.

Some fishermen still set traps to catch fish, but it is rare these days. Dynamite fishing is dangerous and illegal, but still practiced by a few. A yellow powder on the water's surface is evidence of its use. Damaged reefs confirm its use. During World War II, Palauans dynamited the reefs to kill fish and feed the Japanese troops. Palauans lost their lives while dynamite fishing. Abandoned ammunition of unexploded bombs can still be found and used around the Rock Islands and Peleliu. Dynamite kills all sizes and types of fish and destroys the reef and may harm those who use it. Clorox bleach kills fish during the low tides and also destroys the reefs. These practices must be discouraged. Only a desperate man would resort to this today.

Palau has several fishing derbies each year. All fishermen and women get together to test their skills. There are

prize categories for billfish (marlin, sailfish and broad bill swordfish), tuna (yellowfin bigeye and dogtooth), wahoo, mahi mahi, barracuda and giant trevally. These events usually occur over a weekend. At dawn, fisherman head in all directions toward their favorite spots. Some go miles offshore looking for floating logs, good areas to catch billfish and tuna. Others have secret spots by Peleliu. Some fishermen troll along the barrier reefs and reef passes for wahoo, mahi mahi, barracuda and giant trevally. Each fisherman has their special lure, reef and time to catch the big one.

Preparing fish is easy. The fish are so fresh and tasty you need little or no seasoning to bring out the flavor. Fish are barbecued, boiled in soup, fried, baked or eaten raw with some lemon and soy sauce. Any fish can be barbecued on a beach with no preparation. Fish must be cleaned first for other cooking methods. Fish are scaled and the internal organs removed. The liver of the parrotfish and the ripe gonads of any fish are tasty and left inside the fish after cleaning it. A delicious soup can be prepared by adding fish, a pinch of salt, a red pepper and a few fresh leaves of *Spondias pinnata (titimel)* to boiling water. Groupers, parrotfish, and the rabbitfish, *Siganus fuscescens (meas)* are great for soups. The rabbitfish, *Siganus lineatus (klsebuul)* is a great frying fish. Just make some diagonal cuts on either side of the fish and rub a little salt into the cuts. Fry the fish in a skillet with oil for about 5 minutes on either side. You can oven bake large fish like barracudas, groupers and large snappers, with salt, butter and garlic. If you just cannot wait, clean a fish, slice it to bite size pieces and dip it in soysauce for sashimi.

Fishing is an exciting and alluring passion. Why? It's food. It's fun. It's relaxing. It's a challenge! Fishing is people, place, moon and mood. Fisherfolk become awed with a big catch and frustrated with a close call - all within a few hour's time. Fisherfolk have a common bond. There is something genuine and real out on the water. The fresh smell of the open ocean and shallow reef lagoon on a moonless night give credence to this.

As a fishing day ends, the boat must be rinsed thoroughly. The gear is taken out and rinsed with freshwater. The day's catch is shared. Each fish is scaled and gutted. Afterwards, the fishermen linger a bit to chew a betelnut and discuss their catch. Various types of fish behavior and movements are the focus of their conversation. Fishermen do not boast of their abilities because they fish for survival. It is them or the fish. Slowly one by one, they head home. Hot rice or taro is waiting. A few fish are cooked up for soup. Each eats and then finally sleeps to the sound of an early rooster's crow. It is straight forward. It is simple.

REFERENCES

Johannes, Robert E. 1984. *Words of the Lagoon.* University of California Press.

Myers, Robert F. 1989. *Micronesian Reef Fishes.* Coral Graphics

Conversations with Clarence Kitalong and local fishermen.

Diving

To dive in Palau's majestic underwater world is an experience of a lifetime. The photography of Douglas Faulkner brought world recognition to Palau's underwater world during the late 1970's. Before my first journey to Palau, I found Faulkner's book at Oregon State University's library. I thought, "Am I really going to this paradise?" Since then, many famous underwater photographers have filmed here. Descriptions of Palau's underwater are in numerous books, scientific journals and magazine articles. Films and television documentaries by National Geographic, the Discovery Channel and European Broadcasting companies brought Palau's splendor to the world. The recent IMAX Film "The Living Sea," showcased Palau to the world. It's no surprise that Palau is center stage in the scientific and diving communities.

The most recognized dive sites of Palau are within its southern lagoon. Blue Holes, Blue Corner, New Dropoff, and Big Dropoff envelop *Ngemelis* Island. German Channel, Turtle Cove and the Coral Gardens of *Ngedebus* are nearby. The reefs off the tip of Peleliu Island are renown for their strong currents. Peleliu

Corner and Peleliu Express have a strong and unpredictable current that excites experienced divers. These currents can sweep divers out to sea. Along the western barrier reefs of the southern lagoon are Shark City, *Ulong* Channel and *Siaes* Tunnel. The northwestern reefs of *Babeldaob* include the dive sites along *Ngeremlengui* Channel, *Ngardmau* Pass and *Ngaraard* Channel. The southeast reef of *Babeldaob* has Short Dropoff. More and more divers are exploring the reefs of *Babeldaob* and the Northern Lagoon.

The Northern Lagoon has several large barrier reefs that are exciting dive destinations. The rough ocean waters make these areas less accessible and limit the types of marine organisms that can live there. Only during certain times of the year are the ocean waters calm enough for divers to travel North and South of the Main Archipelago of Palau. A visit to the northern Atoll of *Kayangel* requires advance planning and is a great overnight destination. Palauans discourage visitors at the *Ngeruangel* Atoll because it is a bird sanctuary. About 7 miles South of the main archipelago of Palau is the Island of *Angaur. Angaur's* waters are full of large pelagic fish and some sharks.

Sharks of all sizes are an exciting sight
and can always be seen at Blue Corner.

The Southwest Islands lie 200 to 400 miles south of the main archipelago of Palau. The SW islanders have a different language and culture than the rest of Palau. In recent years, chartered live aboard dive boats have scheduled annual trips to the Southwest Islands. These islands are important turtle and seabird nesting sites. These reefs have marine life found nowhere else in the world. Besides natural reef wonders, Palau offers numerous World War II wreck dives around Koror and *Babeldaob.*

Getting there is half the fun. Fast twin engine boats get dive parties from place to place.

PHOTO BY KEVIN DAVIDSON

These haunting Japanese World War II wrecks became living extensions of nearby reefs. The books, "World War II Wrecks of Palau," by Dan Bailey and "Desecrate I, the Shipwrecks of Palau" by Klaus Lindemann extensively cover many of these underwater memorials.

In Palau you can dive throughout the year. Winter and spring are peak diving seasons attracting tourists living in colder places. Many fish are breeding at these times. Summer has calm southwest winds that make *Kayangel* and *Angaur* more accessible and it is possible to see groupers breed in large aggregations in the passes and channels. The fall season has a second, yet smaller peak in breeding activity. The dive sites are dynamic and ever changing all year round. One cannot truly experience Palau without diving its waters. You can simply free dive or use Scuba.

During a typical diving day, your dive guide recommends the best diving options to your group. Meanwhile, the crew readies the gear. The crew loads air tanks and packed lunches onto the boats. The boat is ready to go at

about nine o'clock in the morning and takes 30 to 45 minutes to reach the first dive location. The beauty of the Rock Islands along the way is breathtaking. Dive guides moor the boat to a floating buoy whenever possible to protect the reefs from boat anchors. Everybody gears up, checks their equipment and listens intently to the divemaster's final instructions. Each diver plunges into the water and waits for their buddy just below the surface. Slowly, they descend from the warm

Scuba diving has become a particularly equipment intensive sport. Technological advances have made the sport safer allowing for longer and more comfortable dives.

moist air into the cool blue sea. As they descend, divers look above through a watery blue film of reflected white cumulus clouds. Underwater, the sun's rays diffuse onto the reef and blue sea.

Experienced divers usually take their deep dive first. Deep dives along the outer barrier reefs, passes or the steep vertical walls are fantastic. The walls burst with

every imaginable color of sponge, tunicate and coral. Hundreds of fish fill the vast clear-blue waters. In the midst of their underwater excitement, dive guides remind everyone to stay close together and keep each other within view. The walls serve as a point of reference to keep a diver oriented. Divers drift with the currents if the timing of the tides is right. Otherwise, they must swim against it. Divers must know their limits. New divers find the

"Over the side" as divers put in at Blue Corner.

coral gardens of the shallower lagoon a more relaxing dive. They slowly meander among some of the largest coral on earth. Most dives last about forty-five minutes to an hour. During a slow ascent, a turtle or a blacktip shark may pass by over the reef. In between dives, the Rock Islands and shallower reefs are fun to explore. The second dive at a shallower depth is just as fun. Divers can video or take photographs to document their experience. One last splash breaks divers from the liquid underworld to the surface air. By day's end, joyously pickled divers exclaim over Palau's dazzling salty seaworld.

Divemasters agree with me that some of the best dives and snorkels are not at the most popular dive sites, but at randomly picked areas. The best sources of information about diving are the divemasters. They have many exciting experiences to share. Books written by Nancy Barbour, Mandy Eptison, and Tim Rock & Francis Torbiong describe their varying insights into Palau's diving. These books provide excellent firsthand information and photographs of the dive sites. So let's now take a quick glimpse at some of the diving destinations.

Blue Hole is a cavern containing four holes. These holes open to the surface above. One huge hole at ninety feet opens onto a steep vertical wall. Leopard sharks and large stingrays may sleep inside. Blue Hole is commonly the entrance point for drift dives to Blue Corner during

an outgoing tide. The Hole itself has wire coral and *Tubastrea* coral. Divers experience a wonderful sensation as they slowly descend into these large caverns with the sunlight beaming overhead.

Blue Corner always has sharks, especially the grey reef and whitetip sharks. The whale shark, the scalloped hammerhead, tiger sharks, dogtooth tuna and marlin make occasional appearances. Large schools of barracuda representing three different species: the great barracuda, *Sphyraena*

Blackfin barracuda schools with hundreds of fish are a common sight along the outer edge of the reef and elsewhere in Palauan waters.

One time, six big Napolean wrasses, *Cheilinus undulatus (maml)* came very close to a surprised master diver. Some wrasse weighed over one hundred pounds. The Napolean wrasse is usually a very wary fish and difficult to approach. Now divers feed wrasses and they are less wary. Scientists do not recommend feeding fish, because it alters their natural behavior and makes them more susceptible to predation. At Blue Corner you can see hundreds of fusiliers, *Caesio spp.*, small blue grey triggerfish, *Odonus niger* and pyramid butterfly fish, *Hemitaurichthys polylepis*. The wall of Blue Corner has a variety of sea fans and soft corals

The New Dropoff is just south of Blue Corner on the reefs of *Ngemelis*. This is a favorite dive site for many people because there are plenty of fish during the incoming and outgoing tides. Divers see sharks and large schools of jacks, snappers, butterfly fish and Moorish idols at this site. Big Dropoff is by *Ngemelis* Island's west channel. This is my

PHOTO BY KEVIN DAVIDSON

barracuda (chai), Sphyraena pinguis (meai), blackfin barracuda, *Sphyraena genie (lolou)* and schools of silvery jacks are found here. Hundreds of bigeye scad, *Selar crumenophthalmus (terekrik)* reside here. You are more likely to see predators feeding on bigeye scads at Blue Corner than any other dive site. Predators feeding on the bigeye scads include the jacks, *Caranx melampygus (oruidel)* and *Caranx ignobilis (cheropk),* sharks, small yellowfin tuna, *Thunnus albacares (tekuu)* and the rainbow runner, *Elagatis bipinnulatus (desui).* These predators prey on large schools of the Moorish idols, *Zanclus cornutus* especially from December through April.

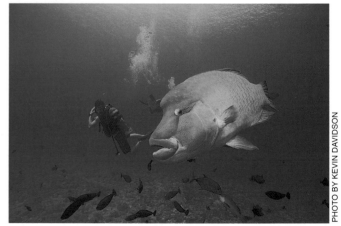

PHOTO BY KEVIN DAVIDSON

Napoleon Wrasse, shown here at Blue Corner, can weight over 400 lbs. (190 kg). They are considered by Palauans to be one of the tastiest fish in the lagoon.

Ngemelis Wall has been rated as one of the best wall dives in the world. Soft corals adorn the sheer rock face in a rainbow of colors.

The Germans built a channel through the reef by *Ngemelis,* known locally as "German Channel." The channel is famous for its cleaning station that attracts the large Manta ray, *Manta alfredi (oklemedaol)* and sharks. Divers descend to a sandy bottom at about forty-five feet and wait behind large coral colonies near the cleaning station. Small blue streaked fish called cleaner wrasse swim overhead advertising their services. Cleaner fish feed upon small parasites that live on large fish. The fifteen to twenty-minute wait is well worth it. It is a thrill when a giant manta swims within a few feet and remains there momentarily while being cleaned. Large sharks wait patiently for a cleaning. Divers gain a new respect for the comparatively tiny, four-inch long cleaner wrasse, *Labroides* spp. that bring giant manta rays and sharks to a halt. It is breathtaking to watch the manta gracefully wave its large wide pectoral fins as it turns away. German Channel has extensive beds of the *Acropora* coral, a giant clam, *Tridacna gigas* (up to four-feet long), hawksbill turtles and garden eels. Schools of the small red snapper, *Lutjanus gibbus (keremlal),* large red snapper, *Lutjanus bohar (kedesau),* black snapper, *Monotaxis* spp. *(kelalk),* goatfish and small yellow snapper are common. Garden eels, the strange looking crocodile fish, *Cymbacephalus beauforti* and the leopard shark, *Stegastoma varium (biall)* thrive here.

favorite snorkeling site. A boat can drop you on the reef in shallow water, so you can snorkel over beautiful coral beds. Once you reach the edge of the reef there is a sheer dropoff of over seven hundred feet. Divers see large sea fan corals and beautiful soft corals here. A snorkeler can enjoy this site just as well as a diver because it is in a more sheltered area of the reef. Sleeping white tip sharks and moray eels hide along the ledges and crevices. Nurse and zebra sharks are common visitors.

German Channel, built during Germany's occupation of Palau to facilitate the transport to Koror of phosphate mined in *Angaur.*

PHOTO BY KEVIN DAVIDSON

Manta ray are often found in German Channel. Also called Devil Rays, these gentle giants
eat only planktonic food items. They can reach 23 ft. (7m) in width and weight over 2800 lbs. (1300 kg).

Turtle Cove, just across from *Ngemelis* Channel, is in a protected area away from the open ocean's pounding waves. Turtles breed and rest at Turtle Cove. An oval shaped hole on top of the shallow reef is your diving entrance. During a slow descent through the hole, a colorful display of soft corals and white sponges hang from the ceiling for your viewing. Grey reef sharks and blacktip sharks may pass by at shallower depths. Small schools of humphead parrotfish, *Bolbometopon muricatum (kemedukl)* often visit. Electric pink fairy basslets, *Pseudanthias pleruotaenia* may be spawning at the cove. During

Dive boats congregate along *Ngemelis* Wall
where they off load divers and snorkelers.

January 1998, three species of parrotfishes: *Scarus psittacus*, *Scarus oviceps* and *Scarus dimidiatus*, and the bird wrasse, *Gomphosus varius* were spawning! The long-jawed mackerel, *Rastrelliger kanagurta (smach)* swam overhead with a wide open mouth feeding upon each puff of gametes. Parrotfish and wrasse tried to chase the mackerel away. Colorful trigger-fish, *Balisotides conspicillum,* schools of pyramid

Turtle Cove. Turtles are excellent swimmers, can reach depths of 200 ft. (60m) and stay submerged for over an hour. Here, a diver closely observes the graceful movement of a young Hawksbill turtle.

PHOTO BY KEVIN DAVIDSON

butterflyfish, *Hemitaurichthys polylepis,* Moorish idols, black snappers, white snappers, *Macolor macularis* and *Macolor niger (kelalk),* barracuda, groupers, soldierfish, *Myripristis* spp. *(bsukl)* and the big eye trevally, *Caranx sexfasciatus (chesuuch)* populate this dive site. An occasional cuttlefish may appear. As you ascend and glance over the reef, there are many small table corals of *Acropora,* a dominant coral of the reef. Triggerfish stand guard near their nests in the sandy patches of shallow water.

Ngedebus is a coral garden where divers are most likely to see a turtle. I saw two hawksbill turtles resting and feeding during my visit in 1998. Nurse sharks, *Nebrius concolor (metmut)* and zebra sharks are at *Ngedebus.*

Peleliu Corner has a pelagic community of sharks, barracuda and surgeonfish and large schools of Moorish idols during the winter. Big tiger sharks or pilot whales, *Globicephala* sp. may make a surprise appearance. Shark City and *Siaes* Tunnel had many sharks, especially grey sharks. Now this is not so. Perhaps over-fishing or a change in their feeding or resting areas occurred at these sites. Divers still enjoy the sea life within the tunnel. Whale sharks, great hammerhead sharks *(ulach)* and even killer whales, *Orcinus orca,* make rare visits to *Siaes* Tunnel. Leopard sharks are occasional visitors in sand pockets along the reef.

Ulong or *Ngerumekaol* Channel is my favorite dive. The uniqueness of *Ulong* Channel is that it does not completely cut through the reef like other channels. It is like a watery blue finger that pokes into the barrier reef, but stops just before the lagoon. Divers can drift through the channel from the inner reef to the

Dive boats cluster along *Ulong* beach between morning and afternoon dives.

Aerial view of *Ulong* Channel. This natural channel extends from the barrier reef to the edge of the inner lagoon. It was formed by erosion as a result of tidal exchange and has a maximum depth of 50 ft. (15m).

PHOTO BY KEVIN DAVIDSON

outer reef. During a drift dive, divers see a clear transition in the reef communities from the inner to outer channel. At the inner end, the giant clam, *Tridacna gigas (otkang)* nestle between the coral. There is one large colony of the coral, *Pavona claves,* that is about fifty feet wide and fifteen feet high! As divers move through the channel, they see continuous plates of the coral, *Turbinaria,* sixty feet long and twenty-five feet high, along the slope. Squirrelfish and soldierfish hide within the *Turbinaria* coral. Dozens of garden eels sway with the currents feeding on what drifts by. If you try to take a closer look the eels quickly retreat into their holes in the sand.

Along *Ulong's* sandy channel bottom there are prickly redfish sea cucumber, *Thelenota ananas (temtamel)* and black teatfish sea cucumbers, *Holothuria nobilis (bakelungal).* In the spring the Titan trigger fish, *Balistoides viridescens (dukl)* aggressively guard their egg in well-spaced nest mounds along the sandy bottom. In December dozens of pink faced triggerfish, *Pseudobalistes flavimarginatus* spawn here. A few humphead parrotfish, *Bolbometopon muricatum (kemedukl)* and the humphead wrasse, *Cheilinus undulatus (maml)* frequent the upper water column or mid water. Hundreds of the black

There are many varieties of grouper that can be seen in *Ulong* Channel. Here a Slender Grouper lurks among the colorful soft coral awaiting its next meal.

PHOTO BY KEVIN DAVIDSON

snapper, *Macolor niger (kelalk)* form one of the largest fish schools of *Ulong* Channel. Large schools of Moorish idols congregate here. At the outer mouth of the channel hundreds of blackfin barracuda, *Sphyraena genie (lolou)* create a schooling whirlpool. You can ascend up through this moving whirl of fish. The grey reef and whitetip sharks slowly cruise by. An occasional leopard or nurse shark may rest on the sandy bottom.

Hundreds of groupers aggregate in *Ulong* Channel every spring and summer. In 1989 I worked with the

Division of Marine Resources and we began to survey the groupers. During three springs and summers we went to count hundreds of groupers that began to aggregate at the channel just after the full moon. While diving along the outer mouth of the channel you can see hundreds of small marbled groupers, *Epinephelus microdon (ksau)*.

PHOTO BY KEVIN DAVIDSON

Small school of Blueline Snappers hover effortlessly in the current.

Modern dive boats need to carry sufficient tanks for large groups on a regular 2-tank dive day.

Over one hundred large blotchy groupers, *Epinephelus fuscoguttatus (temekai)* and spotted groupers, *Plectropomus aerolatus (tiau)* hide under and within the coral heads. Just a day after the new moon the aggregations disperse.

These surveys continued until present and provide new insight into the grouper populations of Palau. *Ulong* Channel is off limits to fishermen.

Short Dropoff is at the elbow of *Uchelbeluu* reef, straight out of *Toachel Mid* Channel (the channel between *Babeldaob* and Koror) heading East. As the boat approaches, a school of spinner dolphins, *Stenella longirostris (demul)* may greet you. The fan coral community is exceptional at Short Dropoff. Fan colors of many sizes and colors are on display vertical row upon row. Like many of the dive sites, it is not uncommon to see fifty species of fish during one snorkel or dive. Schools of barracuda, manta rays, eagle rays and sharks can be found here. Dazzling colors of fusilers, *Caesio* spp., damsel fishes, pomacentrids and the blue *Chromis* fishes accent the waters. Hawksbill turtle and blacktip sharks pass by in the shallow water. On the lowest tides, a wonderful series of sandbars at the back reef area invite the explorer. Sea birds rest along the sandbars' edge. Short Dropoff is also a great night dive.

Lighthouse Channel at the eastern end of *Malakal* harbor is popular for night dives. It is relatively close to the dive shops. Many crustaceans and mollusks are active at night. The small abalone, *Haliotis asinina,* xanthid crabs, small cephalopod, *Euprymna* sp and cowries like *Cypraea chinensis* can be found here. This area is a known feeding ground for dugongs, *Dugong dugon (mesekiu)*, though they are rarely seen by divers.

Ngeremlengui Channel *(Toachel Mlengui)* is a site where the photographer Tim Rock got a rare photograph of the elusive marine mammal, dugong, *Dugong dugon (mesekiu).* There are extensive coral beds of the bowl shaped coral, *Echinopora lamellosa* and the shelf or plate corals, *Turbinaria peltata* and *Pachyseris rugosa.* The gastropod, *Trochus niloticus (semum)* is abundant in this channel. The black teatfish sea cucumber, *Holothuria*

A PERSONAL TOUR OF PALAU

CHAPTER 3: DIVING

49

nobilis (bakelungal) and prickly redfish sea cucumber, *Thelenota ananas (temtamel)* live along the sandy bottom. Humphead wrasse, *Cheilinus undulatus (maml),* humphead parrotfish, *Bolbometopon muricatum (kemedukl),* blue spine unicorn fish, *Naso unicornis (chum),* orange spine unicornfish, *Naso lituratus (cherangel)* and schools of hundreds of red humphead snappers, *Lutjanus gibbus (keremlal)* are part of the diverse fish community at *Ngeremlengui* Channel. The grey reef sharks *(mederart)* seem more aggressive in this channel. Tiger sharks *(mengerengel chedeng)* are periodic visitors outside this channel. *Ngardmau* Channel is a popular spot to observe manta rays. *Ngaraard* Channel also has manta rays. There are large turtles at these northern reefs.

So, that's a quick glimpse of the most popular dive sites waiting for you in Palau! Each dive is a new experience. The reefs and its marine inhabitants are ever changing. So come and discover the reefs of Palau.

I dove Short Dropoff in July of 1998, and saw a disturbing sight. Filamentous algae covered many of the beautiful sea fans and some were partially dead. Then I went to visit several other dive sites in the fall of 1998. At the dive sites we visited, up to 80% of the corals were totally or partially bleaching and about 10% were dead! This coral bleaching was the result of a one to two degree increase in water temperatures caused by a climate change in our region. Corals are very sensitive to slight changes in water temperature. As a result of the increased temperatures, the *zoothanthellae* leave the coral tissue. *Zoothanthellae* are microscopic algae that live in coral tissue. They are plants that use sunlight to make sugars in a process called photosynthesis. The coral feeds on the sugars and the algae are protected within the coral tissue and feed on nitrogenous wastes of the coral. This is called a symbiotic relationship. The coral and algae both benefit by living together. The waters surrounding the coral reefs were murky from the many microscopic algae.

Large multicolored cabbage corals adorn the sides of *Ulong* Channel.

PHOTO BY KEVIN DAVIDSON

The green *zoothanthellae* live within the coral tissue and give corals their beautiful colors. *Zoothanthellae* can also mask colors. When the algae are gone, many kinds of corals are surprisingly different colors. Lavenders, pinks,

bleaching. It saddens me to see so much coral bleaching. Since my visit to Short Dropoff nearly two years ago, scientists estimate that about 30% of Palau's corals died due to this bleaching event. The *Acropora* coral were hit the hardest.

There is recovery occurring on the reefs and the water temperatures are approaching normal levels. There is an urgent worldwide need to stop emitting pollutants into our atmosphere. These pollutants accelerate the warming of our oceans and cause our reefs to die.

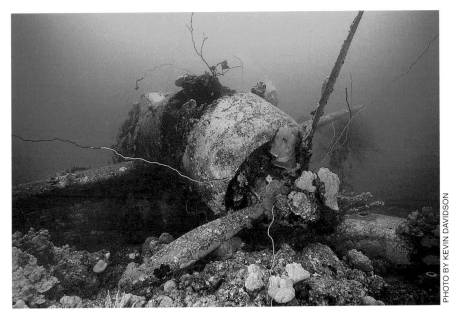

The waters of Palau contain many WWII wrecks. Seen here are the remains of a Japanese 3-seat floatplane.

PHOTO BY KEVIN DAVIDSON

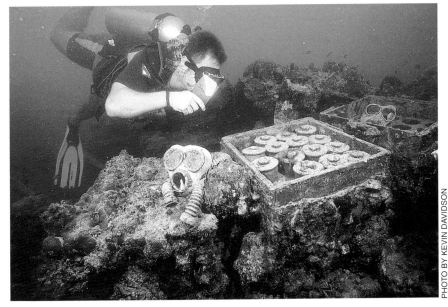

One of many ship wrecks in the Palauan lagoon. This wreck, known locally as the "helmet" wreck, is full of WWII artifacts that can be observed but not taken.

PHOTO BY KEVIN DAVIDSON

Since their first canoe touched ashore, Palauans explored the sea for food. Just a couple of decades ago, recreational diving was uncommon. Historical events slowly changed this. The first diving in Palau with Scuba gear

oranges and yellow tints appear throughout a coral colony and the tips of the branches. Certain soft yellow corals are proliferating over the reef that did not live here before. Some soft corals appear as if they are "melting" and then disintegrating. In my twenty years of diving in Palau, this is my first time to see this phenomenon of massive

began during World War II. Military men trained with Scuba gear. After the war, Scuba gear enabled divers to salvage valuable parts of WWII wrecks in Palauan waters. Among the first Palauan divers were Bena Sakuma and Francis Toribiong. Bena Sakuma's father, Ronald Sakuma, owned the only scrap metal salvaging operation in Palau.

Divers collected fixtures, helmets and guns. They sold much of their metal as scrap. At that time, there was little knowledge of the dangers and safety precautions required for diving. Palauans simply took a tank and dove. There were several fatalities (at least two men died) and serious injuries (lost limbs from explosives). While working for his father one summer, Bena developed the "bends" which partially paralyzed him. Bena's setback did not deter him from his pursuit of diving. After undergoing extensive therapy in Japan, he returned to Palau. In 1974, Bena started the first dive shop in Palau called "Micronesian Aquatics," with just a few dive customers a week.

The early days of Palau's sports diving were special. Most divers came from Guam's military bases and were willing to take high risks for adventure. There was a sense of excitement with just a handful of people involved in this new sport. Micronesian Aquatics used an air compressor at the Division of Marine Resources, the only one on island. Bena and his team co-hosted and cooked for the handful of divers. Giant clamshells were abundant on the beaches and were good serving trays for the famous Rock Island banquets. Bena was and still is a renown storyteller and very knowledgeable about his island. Bena made the concept of drift diving popular. During a drift dive the diver moves effortlessly along the reef in the same direction as the underwater currents. Experienced boat drivers predict where the drift dive ends. The driver waits for the first head to surface before he goes to fetch the dive group.

At the end of the day, dive guides and divers climb aboard for the ride back to Koror.

Francis Toribiong opened up the second dive shop in Palau called Fish n' Fins, in January of 1979. Francis learned Scuba diving and became a certified dive instructor in California. Francis began recreational diving while helping the Sakuma's salvaging business. Eventually, he and his family lived at their shop on M-dock. Francis and his wife Susan combined their skills to develop a thriving business. Francis is knowledgeable about currents and a strong advocate of environmental protection. He has rescued many people at sea when all else failed.

NECO, Ltd. or Ngiratkel Etpison Company began a tour operation out of the Continental Hotel before Scuba diving became popular. They took snorkelers out to tour the Rock Islands. Now, Shallum and his wife, Mandy and the Etpison family have developed NECO Marine Corp., one of the largest diving and tour operations in Palau. Itaru Kishigawa began to develop the Japanese dive trade and started the Carp Resort about the same time as Bena stared his first dive shop. Itaru's daughter, Mari, a dive guide and instructor, assists her father with their large dive operation. Over the past twenty-five years, the diving industry has flourished. What initially started as one compressor and boat has grown into at least fifteen dive operations. Thousands of divers visit each year, generating millions of dollars in revenue. Tourism is Palau's major industry.

The Palau Visitor's Authority sponsored a workshop for dive guides in 1995. During this training Bena Sakuma recalled the risks he and others took while handling

munitions and explosives in the early days of diving. He was lucky to be alive. Bena expressed his concern about the future of Palau's dive sites. Why do we need to keep going to the same places, so far and so fast? There are so many unique reefs, coves, caves and lakes to see nearby. Yet he hesitated when asked to reveal his favorite spots to the dive guides. Would visitors change these fragile ecosystems forever? Bena had bittersweet thoughts of what he worked so hard to start and what it may become. The state governments, the Palau Visitors Authority, the Belau Tourism Association, the Palau Conservation Society and other national and state agencies work together to ensure Palau's diving industry will be sustainable with time.

Yes, Palau is really paradise. A sense of renewal overcomes me with each plunge. A primordial instinct sets in as I move under the sea amongst its mysterious creatures. Palau's rich sea world is filled with every conceivable color, shape and form imaginable. Diving in Palau is truly an experience of a lifetime.

REFERENCES

Bailey, Dan E. 1991. *World War II Wrecks of Palau.*
Barbour, Nancy. 1996. *Palau.*
Lindermann, 1988. *Desecrate I. the Shipwrecks of Palau.*
Mandy Thijssen-Etpison. 1997. *Palau Portrait of Paradise.*
Tim Rock and Francis Toribiong. 1994. *Diving and snorkeling guide to Palau.* Pisces Books. Gulf Publishing Company, Houston Texas.

The Rock Islands

The Rock Islands are wondrous. As your flight approaches the Palauan archipelago the pilot will usually circle the southern portion of the large lagoon to give passengers a casual look at a group of over 400 emerald islands that dapple the crystal blue waters. Stretching from Peleliu to Koror and southeastern *Babeldaob* clusters of islands in a variety of shapes and sizes sit patiently, awaiting your arrival. Welcome to the world famous Rock Islands of Palau.

Visitors are anxious to check in to their hotels and get quickly to their tour operators for a first hand look at these geological marvels. Upon departing from the dock, guests travel by boat through a seemingly endless maze of green and blue wonder. They begin to discover hidden lakes, coves, archways, tunnels and caves. Each Rock Island offers a different surprise. Rock Island forests are probably the last untouched forests of the Pacific. Hundreds of plants and trees are home to birds, bats, skinks and harmless tree snakes. Hundreds of fish, coral and marine life of all kinds fill the lagoon. Green and hawksbill turtles, stingrays, sharks and crocodiles inhabit the waters. It is a natural paradise found nowhere else in the world.

Palauans know their Rock Islands are unique. In 1956, Palauans established the *Ngerukewid* Islands Wildlife Preserve. The *Ngerukewid* Islands are 4.6-miles West of *Mecherchar* Island and 3-miles northeast of *Ngemelis* Island. The *Ngerukewid* Islands are a relatively isolated and unique group of about 37 Rock Islands. The Rock Islands are limestone pinnacles that rise to heights 300-feet above the lagoon. The total Preserve area is close to 3,000 acres and represents 0.2% of Palau's total land mass. A shallow lagoon surrounds the Preserve and a western barrier reef protects it from the open ocean's waves. At least 100 species of plants, 28 species of birds, 80 species of coral, 169 species of fish and 260 other marine invertebrates inhabit this Preserve. The relatively small size and inaccessibility of the *Ngerukewid* Islands discourage inhabitants. No one is allowed into the Preserve area without permission.

Rock Islands are coral pinnacles that rise above sea level. After millions of years of geologic activity, these reefs uplifted out of the water. The larger Rock Islands are actually

World famous 70 Islands and home
of the *Ngerukewid* Islands Wildlife Preserve.
Entrance to this preserve is highly restricted.

continuous uplifted coral reef ridges. Some limestone islands are barrier islands along the outer reefs. The "rock" of a Rock Island is limestone or calcium carbonate. Corals are marine animals that produce an external skeleton of the mineral, calcium carbonate. Close examination of a coral reveals small "polyps" or coral animals living inside tiny depressions of the coral skeleton. It is the coral's external skeleton of calcium carbonate that produces the reef.

The Rock Islands are linked in places by long, steep, heavily vegetated strips on upthrusted limestone.

If you carefully inspect the Rock Islands, you notice a distinctive undercut or notch at sea level. The undercuts range from six to thirty feet in width and give the Rock Islands their mushroom like shape. This unique physical feature is more visible during low tide. As you walk around a Rock Island, you can closely examine the different types of cuts and grooves and the animals found there. The processes of physical, chemical and biological erosion create different types of undercuts and the overall shape of each Rock Island. The physical force of wave action from tidal currents hitting against the limestone wears away the rock and helps to create the undercut. Chemical erosion by carbonic acid slowly dissolves the limestone. Carbonic acid is formed when rainwater runs over fallen leaves that carpet the ground of

Islands are slowly undercut by wave action as well as chemical and biological erosion until, ultimately, they tumble into the lagoon to become a platform for additional coral growth.

every Rock Island. Eventually this water finds its way to the sea. The acid laden rainwater is lighter than saltwater and floats on the top forming a corrosive layer that comes in contact with the islands limestone walls, slowly eating them away. Saltwater alone may dissolve the limestone. Marine mollusks biologically erode the limestone. Chitons (primitive, flattened mollusks with 8 shell valves) and snails eat algae growing on the rock islands and slowly scrap away limestone. No one knows which process, physical, chemical or biological erosion plays the

greatest role in the creation of the undercuts. The undercut is the demarcation between the forest and the sea. Occasionally you see a gap in the forest where a large tree could no longer hold up its weight on the harsh substrate and dropped into the lagoon below. Sometimes the overhanging portion of a rock island becomes too heavy

CHAPTER 4: THE ROCK ISLANDS

A PERSONAL TOUR OF PALAU

and falls into the lagoon. Undercuts, ledges and caves at high elevations occur along the periphery of Rock Islands. Each Rock Island uplifted differently over geological time.

Rock Island forests touch the sea. The low-lying branches adapt by growing out and expanding horizontally just above the high tide mark. Green ferns, browned by the sun and sea, hang over the edges. The trees cling to the rock in a tangled web of overlapping and far reaching roots. A precarious life just above the sea. While traveling through the emerald islands, you see magnificent hues and textures of rich vegetation. The limestone mushrooms are cathedrals of cellulose and chlorophyll. Nature dressed the forests in greens upon greens with tints of yellow and brown. Leaves of all shapes and sizes: shiny and dull, thin and succulent, serrated and smooth edged leaves dress tree limbs. Over a hundred kinds of plants thrive in the Rock Islands.

Cliff habitats are nearly vertical outcrops with slopes

Bare limestone faces are common in the Rock Islands. In some instances it is the result of the collapse of an outcropping.

Perfect example of the undercut found on most Rock Islands. The overhanging portion may reach lengths of 30 ft. (approx. 10 meters).

exposed to salt spray. Visitors come face to face with shear limestone cliffs. Soil is nearly absent. The plants adapt to salt spray and dryness. The shrub *Pemphis acidula (ngis)* thrives here. The pitcher plant *Nepenthes mirabilis (meliik)* grows along the outer edges in a tangled web of vines. One white flower punctuates the grey green cliffs.

Colorful ferns cover the ground in shades of green and brown. Orchids cling to many trees. The endemic white lily, *Bikkia palauensis (rur)* highlights the limestone rocks. The lily has a large trumpet-like white flower and wonderful perfumed fragrance. I consider this lily the "flower of the Rock Islands."

On exposed outcrop and ridges, the endemic palm, *Gulubia palauensis (bochela uchererak)* pokes out from the limestone. The Greater Sulphur-crested Cockatoo, *Cacatua galerita (iakkotsiang)* eats the heart of this palm, evenually killing the tree. The cockatoo is not a native bird, it was introduced to Palau as a pet. The immense hardwood, *Intsia bijuga (dort)* stands out with its gnarled branches that reminds me of Halloween night. The most abundant tree is the "Rock Island guava," *Eugenia*

Vegetation lines most sandy beaches. Many of the coconut palms started from sea born coconuts that drifted ashore from neighboring islands.

(korrai) forms dense thickets. The coconut tree, *Cocos nucifera (lius)* is the universal tree of all island shores. Palauans use the coconut tree for building, weaving, food, oil, drink and medicine. The large tree *Hernandia sonora (doko)* has fruits that resemble small lanterns. The big tree *Pongamia pinnata (kisaks)* has lavender flowers. The shade tree *Calophyllym inophyllym (btaches)* has sweet scented flowers with white petals and golden pollen. The large tree *Barringtonia asiatica (bduul)* has gorgeous flowers, each an explosion of hundreds of lavender filaments dipped in golden pollen.

Farther inland you may find the wax apple tree, *Eugenia malaccensis (kidel)* that has edible fruits. Women use the leaves of the *Pandanus* trees, *Pandanus dubius* and *Pandanus tectorius (ongor)* to weave baskets and mats. The rubbery vine *Polyscias grandiflora (bungaruau)* hangs from many trees. The stout cycad, *Cycas circinalis (remiang)* and the famed

Coconuts can drift for many days and travel hundreds of miles.

reinwardtiana (kesiil). Pigeons eat its orange guava-like fruit. This medium sized tree with white flowers is everywhere.

Trees and shrubs line the Rock Island shores. The small heliotrope tree, *Tournefortia argentea (rirs)* attracts butterflies when in blossom. The shrub, *Scaevola sericea*

medicine tree, *Aidia cochincninensis (kerumes)* abound. The tree *Aglaia palauensis (meseoes)* has terminal leaf buds that remind me of praying hands. The trees *Premna obtusifolia (chosm)* with its black berries and *Guettarda speciosa (blau)* with its fragrant white tubular flowers thrive. The poison tree, *Semecarpus venensosus (tonget)* has

a bleeding black sap that when touched causes a painful rash.

Rock Islands rise upward to three hundred feet. (Imagine! These islands were once underwater reefs.) Trees living 100 feet above the waterline can grow to heights of 90 feet. While scanning each island you notice the same types of plants from the top to bottom. The many species of fig trees, *Ficus.* spp. *(lulk)* are the largest trees of the forest and have amazing buttressed roots. The gnarled Halloween-like branches of the ironwood, *Intsia bijuga (dort)* are striking in form. The brown leafed tree *Pouteria obovata (chelangel)* is easy to spot. The leaves of the lily *Dracaena*

Dense vegetation on sandy beach.

multiflora (orredakl) radiate out in all directions like the spines of a sea urchin. The trunks of the wind twisted ironwood tree *Causarina equisetifolia (ngas)* erupt straight out of the rock. Forests of ironwood trees thrive on many islands. The ironwood's brown needle-like leaves create a soft carpet for your feet. Campers may gather the needles to make a soft mattress to sleep upon. The *Pandanus tectorius (ongor)* has sharp edged leaves that fold down towards the sea.

During the day, skinks and geckos climb the trees and coconut crabs rustle in forest leaves. A dozen birds and two kinds of bats dwell within the limestone forests. Noddies, terns, fruitdoves, swiftlets, kingfishers and starlings fly in the sky. The nests of the brown noddy, kingfisher and white-tailed tropic bird are visible from the lagoon. Birds cry out from their nests on the cliffs. They circle above, watching your every move while swooping lower and lower with each circle they make. The most graceful and attractive bird of the Rock Islands is the white-tailed tropic bird, *Phaethon lepturus (dudek).* Dozens of tropic birds may rest on the lagoon waters, sheltered from the wind by the Rock Islands. The Palau fruit bat, *Pteropus pelewensis (olik)* is the Rock Island's "mammal of the sky." A bat in flight gracefully moves its large black wings

Rock Island gecko climbs the rough bark of an ironwood tree.

Tropical bird flies gracefully on the wind before coming to land in the upper branches of large trees. Tropical birds will venture 50 to 60 miles (approx. 90 km.) from shore and are welcome sights to sailors eager to find land.

across the blue sky. Bats fly from tree to tree searching for fruit. Large bats roost in the Rock Islands of *Airai* and Koror. Crabs like *Graspus* sp., clusters of white ribbed *Nerite* snails and the unusual chitons are along the intertidal zone within the notched and pitted edges of the islands. An occasional coral snake, *Laticuada colubrina (mengerenger)* may move along the Rock Island's edge. The dorsal fin of a young blacktip shark may move in your direction as you wade in the shallow waters along the shore.

The lagoon is teeming with marine life. Thickets of branching coral, *Acropora* spp., and the massive coral heads of *Porites* spp. dominate the quiet lagoons. The branch tips of *Acropora* coral are tints of pink, yellow and lavender. Some coral colonies are completely blue. The black damselfish, *Stegastes lividus* dashes in and out scaring away hungry juvenile parrotfish and wrasse. The damselfish is a "farmer fish" that feeds on algae. It maintains an algae garden within the staghorn coral, *Acropora* species. Damselfish lay demersel eggs near its algal garden. This highly territorial fish aggressively protects both its eggs and algal food. The unwelcome crown-of-thorns, *Acanthaster planci* feeds on corals, leaving behind a telltale trail of bleached white coral skeletons. Red algae cling to dead *Acropora* branches. Embedded in the hemispherical-shaped *Porites* are bright blue and green giant clams, *Tridacna crocea (oruer), mytilid* clams, *Septifer bilocularis* and the colorful Christmas tree worms, *Spirobranchus giganteus.* Shallow waters shaded by forest trees have corals dressed in iridescent greens, reds and purples. Some corals have cream-colored centers. Colorful tunicates and sponges thrive in shady spots. Schools of black surgeonfish and butterfly fish come and go. A

few gobies poke their heads in and out of holes in the sand. Seagrass beds of short grasses (*Syringodium isoetifolium, Cymodocea rotundata* and *Halophila ovalis*) grow in the sand. The seagrasses release numerous white pollen grains that move as white waves with the surface currents. Grey sheets of the sponge, *Phyllospongia* sp. can be found. On certain days, giant clams, corals and sea cucumber release pulses of white clouds filled with eggs and sperm. One afternoon, I saw a sea cucumber poised half-upright right next to a giant clam and both were releasing puffs of white clouds in asynchronous rhythm.

Sea grass beds near Peleliu.

Corals exposed by an unusually low tide radiate with color.

There are many special "out of the way" places to explore. Trails lead up to old Japanese posts along the ridges of some islands. Small hidden caves are common. There are over 70 marine lakes throughout the Rock Islands. These hidden lakes are home to many unusual marine creatures. The only lake open to the public is Jellyfish Lake *(Ongeim'l Tketau Uet)* on *Eil Malk* Island.

There are many secluded coves throughout the maze of Rock Islands. Narrow passageways lead into the coves. Shallow sandy waters surrounded by limestone forests isolate these coves from the rest of the lagoon. Upon entry into some coves, a stingray, shark, turtle and even a crocodile may suddenly appear! Once within a cove, it is very quiet and serene. Schools of sardines and fish swim among the sea grass and corals. Mangroves hug the shoreline of some coves and marine lakes.

There are many caves to explore above and below the lagoon. The most attractive feature of caves is the naturally forming stalactites suspended from the ceiling and walls. These icicle shaped formations of crystalline calcium carbonate form by the dripping of water through overlying limestone. Chandelier Cave of *Ngarol* Island is famous and has five chambers to explore. Access by an underwater tunnel requires scuba

"Fern Grottos" because large ferns grow among the enormous precariously hanging stalactites. Some tourists may don their mask and snorkel and explore the watery edges of the cave. Burial caves like *Olekul ra Risong* have remnants of pottery and bones and are off limits to visitors. There are several burial caves that most Palauans do not enter out of respect for their ancestors.

The beauty of the Rock Islands is inviting. In the past, Palauans lived on some of the larger Rock Islands. The smallest Rock Islands are barely large enough to stand on. Visitors come to share a picnic, snorkel, swim or just find a peaceful quiet place to rest. Local residents have built small

Randomly discarded leaves form floating mosaics in an infinite variety of contrasting colors.

Many Rock Islands harbor secluded coves rimmed with trees and shrubs.

gear. Good skin divers can swim through without scuba gear. Many of the caves are above water and easily accessible. Tourists enjoy exploring the inner chambers. Once within a cave, this secret dark place echoes with the sounds of bats and swiftlets flying overhead. Some caves are partially submerged and accessible by boat. So rather than visit dark damp places, tourists go to many well-lit caves without leaving the boat. I call some of the caves

shelters on some Rock Islands. Palauans hunt fruit bats and pigeons in the Rock Island forests. Residents camp for a few nights and enjoy barbecued fish. Popular tourist spots have crowds of boats and people. Only selected areas of the Rock Islands

in Koror State are open for tourist activity. These islands include *Ulong, Ngchus, Ngeanges* or NECO Island, parts of *Euidelchol* or Clam City, *Ngeremeaus*, Jellyfish Lake at *Mecherachar, Babelomekang* (or Two Dog Beach) and *Eoulomekang* area. Coastal areas of *Ngeremdiu*, beach areas of *Ngereblobang*, parts of *Ngebusech* called *Bkulotuut* and *Ngerchong* are accessible to tourists. Koror State requires tour groups to obtain Rock Island Use and Dive Permits depending on the activities planned. The local government uses the fees from the permits to clean and manage the Rock Islands. Tour companies plan the destinations for their guest. Local residents and tour guides check with Koror State on a regular basis because restricted areas may change from year to year.

During a Rock Island tour, visitors may explore more than one Rock Island. Most of the accessible Rock Islands are along the western side of the southern lagoon. The large Rock Island of *Ngeruktabel* divides the Rock Islands on the East and West sides of the Southern lagoon. *Ngeruktabel* Island is a continuous uplifted reef ridge. The large lagoon and barrier reef protect the western side of the southern lagoon. The waters here are usually calmer and easier to travel than the eastern side. Rock Island tours may begin along the western side of the southern lagoon heading South. The tour may include visits to Soft Coral Arch, the Natural Archway, Cemetery Reef of *Olkeriil* Island and *Ngchus* Island. Then you may pass through *Kekerei Toi*, a narrow passageway and head farther West towards *Ulong* Island.

Tours may bypass *Ulong* Island and continue south to a midway area between the large Rock Islands of *Ngeruktabel* and *Mecherchar.* This midway area has

Many Rock Islands are pock marked with caves above and below the water.

Aerial view of *Ngerchong* Island at the edge of the lagoon on the Eastern side of the Rock Islands.

a cluster of smaller Rock Islands that include *Ngeanges* or Neco Island, *Ngermeaus* and *Euidelchol* Island or Clam City. Visitors spend the entire day in this area. They can picnic, snorkel and explore each island. Sometimes tours bypass this midway point and continue further South to a group of Rock Islands that include *Babelomekang* or *Eoulomekang*. These Islands have shade trees, picnic areas, beaches and reefs to explore all day. Divers or snorkelers picnic here after visiting the reefs of *Ngemelis* Island or German Channel.

Along the eastern side of the southern lagoon we find *Ngeremdiu* Beach, part of *Ngeruktabel* Island and Jellyfish Lake on *Mecherchar* Island. So a tour may stop early to snorkel, explore and picnic at *Ngeremdiu* Bay and continue farther South to *Ngeroblobang* Island for similar activities, then visit Jellyfish Lake in the late afternoon. *Ngerchong* Island is South of *Mecherchar* Island along the eastern side of the southern lagoon. There are beautiful coral gardens to explore here. Tours spend an entire day at *Ngerchong* Island. So now you know some of your Rock Island tour options. Let's take a closer look at some of these special sites.

Soft Coral Arch is a famous underwater archway that is part of a Rock Island cluster to the West of *Ngeruktabel* Island. When you approach the archway, at first you

think you are heading straight into a Rock Island. Then you realize there is a small archway that is half-visible at the water's surface. There is a mooring rope for the boats. Schools of blue fusiliers, *Caesio* sp. surround the boat, searching for tidbits of food. In deeper waters there may be a large humphead

View of Ngerchong Island from sea level surrounded by sparkling blue water.

Ngermeaus Island is a favorite snorkeling and picnic beach as well as a frequent stopping place for tour boats.

wrasse, *Cheilinus undulatus (maml),* a fast moving jack, *Caranx melampygus (oruidel)* and perhaps a grouper fish hiding within the corals. The archway itself provides a spectacular array of soft corals just a few feet below the surface. The luxuriant growth of soft corals,

Babelomekang Island, popularly known by tourists as "two dog island."

of the nearby reef. Most visitors linger by the arch itself. Others may wander under the arch that leads into an open cove facing westward. Along the right side of the Rock Island, there are a variety of iridescent corals of the Favid family in the shallow areas shaded by the overhanging forest. Other coral encountered include the plates of *Echinopora mammiformis* and the mushroom coral, *Fungia.* The dominant corals are 5 varieties of *Porites.* Soft coral arch is a busy place with up to 12 boats of tourists a day. Sometimes I notice more sediment on the shallower reef areas. Yet I continue to see young corals recruit into this area. The twice daily exchange of nutrient rich tidal waters helps explain the proliferation of soft corals in this archway.

Dendronephthya spp. showcase every hue of a pastel rainbow. Within the archway dwells the cock's comb oyster, *Lopha cristagalli,* with a distinctively jagged shell.

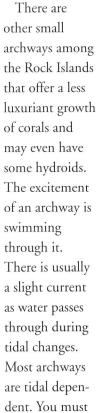

There are other small archways among the Rock Islands that offer a less luxuriant growth of corals and may even have some hydroids. The excitement of an archway is swimming through it. There is usually a slight current as water passes through during tidal changes. Most archways are tidal dependent. You must

NECO Island, a less frequented and secluded place to relax the afternoon away.

The giant clam, *Tridacna squamosa* with its large leaf-like flutes may be present. Sea whips, *Cirripathes* sp. stick out

swim through during high tide or risk scraping against stinging coral during low tides. (Soft coral arch is less

tidal dependent than others areas because it is in deeper water.) This slightly faster current carries small particulate matter that is food for soft corals, fan corals and sponges.

During the high tide you must swim underwater a few minutes and may need scuba gear to do so. Underwater tunnels connect lakes and coves. These tunnels can be a bit scary as there is less light and visibility may be poor.

The Natural Archway is a highlight of a Rock Island tour. After a visit to Soft Coral Arch, the tour boat travels around *Ongrael* Island towards the large natural arch of stone. This Rock Island is the Natural Archway. Tourists stop and climb up onto the island for a photograph under the arch. Your tour can continue south of *Ongrael* Island towards Cemetery Reef.

Cemetery Reef is part of the fringing reef of *Olkeriil* Island, which is South of *Ongrael* Island. "Cemetery" refers to large slabs of concrete that are underwater.

Ulong is often the place to have lunch and rest between morning and afternoon dives.

Ngchus Island is a reclusive spot featuring remains of a Japanese WWII facility, airplane wreckage and the ruins of an old bridge.

Japanese scientists made these cement slabs and placed them here during a scientific experiment involving corals. My last visit here was June 1998; there was a large humphead wrasse, *Cheilinus undulatus* (maml) and schools of damselfish that tourists fed. Along the reef there were rich beds of coral and giant clams imbedded in the rocks.

Ngchus Island is among a cluster of Rock Islands near the Natural Arch and Cemetery Reef area. The Japanese raised pearl oysters and sea turtles here long ago. Clarence's great uncle worked here. Remnants of old foundations and a stone pier are still there. There is a shelter for picnics and a large island to explore. Forests shade the fringing reefs. As you snorkel you will find parts of an old Japanese plane that crashed during World War II.

Ulong Island consists of six Rock Islands and four patches of reef. It is hard to miss this large island group. It

Natural Arch is a scenic wonder often visited by tour boats.

memorials of historic events. *Ulong* Island can be a great educational tour for all. Palauans can tell you the history of the shipwreck of Captain Wilson in 1783 and its impact on Palau. Some tourists hike over the Rock Island ridge to the cove where Captain Wilson set up camp and rebuilt his ship. It is a treacherous walk

lies along the barrier reef and is farther west than most Rock Islands. Tours may head straight for *Ulong's* outer reefs. The waters are sometimes rough along the way. The inner and outer reefs have a high diversity of fish and coral and many giant clams. *Ulong* Island has beautiful beaches and reefs, remnants of old villages, caves and

over limestone. Scattered pottery shards lie along the beach as evidence of a village past. Caves along the northwestern side have old paintings on the walls. The climb is up a steep cliff and not recommended for everyone. The eastern shore has a long beach that also serves tourists. Turtles nest on eastern beaches.

Palauan "summer house" at *Ngchus*.

Ngeanges Island or NECO Island is a Rock Island that lies North of *Mecherchar* and midway in the Southern lagoon. Boats pass by while crossing from the West to East side of the lagoon. Megapode birds nest on this island. One time we watched as a megapode flew from shore as our boat approached. The shoreline has the shade tree *Calophyllum inophyllum (btaches),* coconut trees and bushes of *Tournefortia argentea (rirs).* There are scattered pottery shards on the shore. During a snorkel I saw *Turbinaria* corals, different types of *Porites* coral. Small groups of

juvenile parrotfish, goatfish and rabbitfish foraged food along the reef. I saw a school of convict tangs, *Acanthurus triostegus triostegus* (yes, it is a double spelling) and a couple of triggerfish, *Rhinecanthus verrucosa* swam by. A solitary triggerfish, *Pseudobalistes* sp. guarded its nest. The highlight of one snorkel was a little yellow boxfish, *Ostracion cubicus* hiding in the coral.

Ngermeaus Island is a smaller island with a large beach that reaches out into the lagoon. This is a very popular lunch spot for Rock Island tour groups. It has a shelter and a large sandy beach. Tourists snorkel out along its fringing reef. There are large areas of *Acropora* coral along this reef. We camped at this island once and found a big coconut crab in the early evening.

Ngchelobel Island or Clam City is a 5-minute boat ride from *Ngermeaus*. A Palauan family owns the beach area, so they restrict the area from time to time. We often snorkel first at *Ngermeaus*, have lunch and then go visit the clam farm at *Ngchelobel* Island. Clam City is one place that you will see six species of giant clams during a 45-minute snorkel. The giant clam *Tridacna gigas (otkang)* is the largest clam in the world! This clam grows to 6-feet in length but most of the clams are about 3-feet long. The giant clam *Tridacna derasa (kism)* grows to a foot and a half, has a very low sculptured shell and variable colored mantle. The giant clam *Tridacna squamosa (ribkungel)* grows just over a foot in length and has

Tourists relax and eat lunch at *Ngermeaus*.

large leaf-like flutes on the surface of its shell. The common giant clam *Tridacna maxima (melibes)* grows just under a foot in length and has well-developed concentric growth folds on its shell. The smallest giant clam *Tridacna crocea (oruer)* grows to about 4 inches, has very short flutes on its shell and lives embedded in coral rock. Another genus of giant clam, *Hippopus hippopus (duadeb)* grows to just over one foot in length. You can recognize

Tranquil beauty of random vegetation on the beach at Ngerong Island.

this clam by its brownish mantle with fine white lines over the surface. A stop at Clam City is well worth it and a guarantee to see hundreds of these phenomenal clams.

The excitement of the clams usually overwhelms visitors. Other marine life inhabits the reef. The reef supports a large variety of corals. Vase sponges are common. Parrotfish like *Scarus dimidiatus* and clown fish like *Amphiprion* sp. live at Clam City reef. Along the sandy reef flat is the Picasso triggerfish, *Rhinecanthus* sp. Nuisance pink damselfish, *Dischistodus perspicillatus* nip at your mask. Visitors may explore the beach and a hidden cove behind the beach of Clam City. They find coconut trees, wax apple trees, the orange blossomed tree *Cordia subcordata (badirt)* and the hardwood *Intsia bijuga (dort)*. In the cove there are mysterious algal mats shaped like the mushroom coral, *Fungia.* The Western side of *Ngchelobel* has seven beaches during low tide. These beaches are for local residents.

Ngeremdiu Beach, part of *Ngeruktabel* Island, has a long stretch of beach and forested shoreline to investigate. While snorkeling you may sight a few sharks in this area. Along the outer reef there is an old War World II plane that is still intact. Tours stop first at the plane wreck during high tide. Tourist can swim around and above it. The plane is partly exposed during low tide. The outer reefs have many top shells, *Trochus niloticus (semum).* There is wave action on the reefs outside. Most tour groups head to the beach areas after a visit to the plane wreck. They spend the rest of their day exploring the beach and nearby reefs.

Mecherchar or *Eil Malk* Island is just South of

Ngeruktabel Island. The famous Jellyfish Lake or *Ongeim'l Tketau Uet* is on this island. There is a floating dock at the shoreline so boats don't have to use their anchors. The hike into the lake takes about 15 minutes. The trail has educational boards and tree markers along the way. It is a fun hike. The lake's entrance is on the northwestern side. Tourists visit Jellyfish Lake in late afternoon because the jellyfish concentrate at the northern end at this time. Jellyfish migrate with the sun from the east side to the west side during the day. Another floating pier provides access into the lake. Tourists swim straight out for about 10 minutes. Within a minute of your snorkel you often see jellyfish. Gelatinous cream orange *Mastigias* sp. jellyfish and white moon jellyfish, *Aurelia* sp. pulsate rhythmically around you. The jellyfish do not sting, so you are safe in their presence. Snorkelers swim until the numbers of jellyfish overwhelm them. There are thousands of jellyfish! They remain amongst the jellyfish, gazing at these wondrous creatures. As they swim back they may notice the large mangrove trees along the edge of the lake, the Rock Island forests surrounding them and birds calling out overhead.

Ngerchong Island, just South of *Mecherchar* Island, has a beautiful coral garden. You can snorkel or dive this area. This was the first Rock Island I ever camped on back in 1977. I have camped there a half a dozen times since. Back then the area was renown for both its coral and the large fish populations. There was only one house. We slept in an open shelter. The only time I carried a speargun was when I first camped at *Ngerchong.* The large

Adjacent Rock Islands provide a relaxing view from *Ngermeaus* Beach.

schools of humphead parrotfish and wrasse and sharks intimidated me. I was too naive to know that these large schools of fish would not hurt me. They seemed curious about my presence. I remember lines and lines of a variety of parrotfish, surgeonfish and snappers. The fishermen in our group caught them within a few hours. Today you will not see as many of these large fish. Past memories of *Ngerchong* camping trips are still vivid in my mind. This reef area is still famous for its coral gardens.

Ngeroblobang beach is part of *Mecherchar* Island. There is a shelter at this site. The plants along the shore include coconuts, the hardwood *Intsia bijuga (dort)* and a special type of breadfruit tree.

Omekang Island is actually a cluster of Rock Islands that include *Babelomekang* (upper *Omekang* Island) and *Eoulomekang* (lower *Omekang* Island) Islands. *Babelomekang* or "Two Dog Beach" is home to two dogs. *Babelomekang* Beach is in a protected area surrounded by neighboring islands that you can walk to during low tide.

There are over fifty species of corals to view and hundreds of fish. During low tide, tourists explore the nearby islands. Snorkelers can either swim around the island during high tide or wade around the islands during low tide. Tour boats travel through these islands on their way to German Channel and the reefs of *Ngemelis*.

Ngercheu Island or Carp Island is just North of Peleliu and owned by a clan in Koror. On its western reef is Turtle Cove, a popular dive site that had many turtles. Carp Island offers overnight accommodations. Guests enjoy days of diving, snorkeling and exploring the Rock Island. Upon arrival, the boat docks along a lovely boardwalk. Visitors slowly walk across the boardwalk, gazing at the lovely island before them. A large expanse of sand beach becomes exposed during low tide. Small cottages are interspersed between coconut trees along the beach front and further inland. A mangrove fringe borders the far end of *Ngercheu's* protected sandy cove. The island rises high above the lagoon and has many old

Dive boats and tour boats at *Babelomekang*.

remnants of past activities. It is customary to burn and eat coconut meat on this island in respect of the clan's ancestors.

Several Rock Islands are within the southeastern lagoon of *Babeldaob* and are part of *Airai* State. Tour groups explore the Yapese money on *Metuker ra Bisech* Island. The boat approaches a shelter and stone dock. The 10-minute walk starts out over steep terrain then levels off before more steep terrain. There is a hand rail to guide visitors. The Yapese money is about 10 feet in diameter.

There is a cluster of Rock Islands near *Metuker ra Bisech* Island with coves and caves to explore. Within *Airai* Bay is *Ngkesill* Island. This island has a beach and shelter and an active megapode nest. Piles of shells of the giant clam, *Hippopus hippopus (duadeb)* and the spider mollusk, *Lambis lambis (sang)* are on the beach. The rabbitfish, *Siganus fuscescens (meas)* come near *Ngkesill* Island to spawn every spring. During the rabbitfish spawning season, Palauans cannot fish by *Ngekesill* Island. *Ngeream* Island is home to one of the largest bat colonies in Palau. There are many large caves, coves and mangrove channels to explore in *Airai*.

The Rock Islands are wondrous. Each island has its own special fringe of reef and forest. Their forests touch the sea connecting life above and below the lagoon. Each

Big sandy beach serves as play area as well as arrival and departure point on the eastern end of *Babelomekang* Island.

visit to the luxuriant soft corals, the giant clam farm and the unique marine lakes filled with jellyfish is awe-inspiring. There are still so many mysterious creatures and places yet to explore among the Rock Islands. We enjoy the Rock Islands throughout our lives. Yet we can never see it all in one lifetime. With each visit the maze of islands becomes more familiar. We visit our favorite Rock Islands time and time again. During camp outs we awaken to a morning's tide bringing small schools of silversides and mullets towards shore. The water lifts flower blossoms from the sand and spreads them over the lagoon. Birds sing sweet melodies. An occasional fisherman stalks a silver cloud of sardines. After our visit we travel homeward with the tide and sunset. The evening's light slowly silhouettes the Rock Islands against the pastel sky.

REFERENCES

Birkeland C. and H. Manner. 1989. *Resource survey of the Ngerukewid Islands Wildlife Preserve.* Republic of Palau. South Pacific Regional Environment Programme.

Ngerel a Biib. No.7&8. 1998. *Newsletter of the Palau Conservation Society.*

Visit with Koror Rangers 1998.

the green canopy of the limestone forest. Ferns carpet the floor interspersed with large buttressed trunks. The brown undersides of the leaves distinguish the *Pouteria obovata (chelangel)* tree. The tree *Trema orientalis (chelodechoel)* is full of black fruit. The large fig tree *Ficus microcarpa (lulk)* has octopus like roots that cling to the rocks and other trees. The fig tree slowly strangles life

The marine lakes vary in size. Smaller lakes are the size of a small farm pond. Larger lakes can be as long as 1.25 miles.

Photo by Coral Reef Research Foundation

There are approximately 70 marine lakes in the Rock Islands. The lakes are very different from each other in terms of the marine life found in them.

water in these lakes is brackish. Some enclosed lakes with less tidal exchange have stratified layers of water. The top layers of water are usually brackish, poor in nutrients and contain high levels of oxygen. The bottom layers have less oxygen, more nutrients and high levels of sulfur, nitrogen and phosphorous. Organic material from leaves and dead organisms form layers on the bottoms of deep lakes with limited exchange. The physical and chemical characteristics of each lake determine what types of plants and animals can make a lake their home.

Hiking into Jellyfish Lake takes about fifteen to twenty minutes. Visitors climb over a steep ridge on the ocean side, walk about 100 meters through jungle along the ridge crest and descend down a steep slope to the lake. When you start to walk, within seconds you slip under

from immense trees that once supported them. Palauans harvest the hardwood *Intsia bijuga (dort)* for its strong durable wood. The tree *Pongamia pinnata (kisaks)* has dark, crinkled leaves and lavender flowers that dance in the wind. The mountain guava tree, *Eugenia reinwardtiana (kesiil)* are everywhere. Their white flowers turn into plump orange fruit, a treat for the birds. The Palauan apple tree, *Eugenia javanica (rebotel)* has large

dark green leaves with medicinal qualities and edible fruits. The stiff and sharp edged leaves of *Pandanus aimiriikensis (chertochet)* scratch you as you pass. The endemic poison tree *Semecarpus venenosus (tonget)* has a pale colored trunk with bleeding black sap. It has elongated leaves, shiny on the surface with a dull underside. A miserable rash usually results if you touch or brush against them. Symptoms appear as itchy blisters that can last up to a week and resemble a bad case of poison ivy. Surprisingly I have not heard of a case of *tonget* rash from a tourist! Yet, several research teams had members contract the notorious "*tonget* rash."

Jellyfish Lake.

There is no clear vantage point to view Jellyfish Lake along the existing trail. Once you reach the western end of the lake you can rest a moment and gaze towards the narrow channel leading into the lake. Snorkeling through the 4-foot deep channel, you see mangrove roots along your right side and rocks on your left. Large rocks lie within the channel, so watch yourself. Colorful benthic communities cling to the lake's edge attached to roots or the bank itself. Clusters of black mytilid mussels, green algae, sponges, and the soft white sea anemones, *Entacmaea medusivora* accent the mangrove roots with dazzling colors. The lake's water is a turbid blue green. You may stop and look up to scan the lake's surface. The lake is about 420-meters long by 150-meters wide. Floating leaves and flowers from the trees above dress the water's surface and lake floor. As you resume your snorkeling, you begin to see the jellyfish. At first you see one, then two, then dozens, then hundreds and finally

thousands of jellyfish. Soon millions of jellyfish envelop you, each lost in its own liquid waltz. The late afternoon light captures the graceful motion of their golden bodies like open parasols coming to life.

The mysterious non-stinging jellyfish, *Mastigias* sp. and the white, translucent moon jellyfish, *Aurelia* sp. are both members of the Class *Scyphozoa*. The *Mastigias* sp. of Jellyfish Lake have stinging cells called nematocysts that have lost most of their potency. While spending a full day filming inside Jellyfish Lake I began to feel some stinging around the neck of my wet suit. I am not sure what caused it, whether it was the jellyfish or something else in the water. Scientists believe it was probably the *Mastigias* sp. jellyfish that stung me. The *Mastigias* jellyfish stings and kills copepods for food and can give us a slight sting on our lips and neck. The creamy *Mastigias* sp. contain small, one-celled algae called *zooxanthellae* within their tissue. These one-celled algae need sunlight to produce sugars in a process called photosynthesis. The jellyfish rely on these sugars for food. The tissue of the jellyfish protects the algae within. This relationship of mutual benefit between the algae and jellyfish is called symbiosis. The moon jellyfish *Aurelia* sp. is a carnivore that feeds on microscopic crustaceans called copepods. Dr. Michael Dawson has finished molecular work that indicates there may be three species of *Aurelia* jellyfish: a lake, a cove and lagoon/ocean variety.

The jellyfish swim to the place with the best sun exposure. Jellyfish move with the sun each day. One morning we swam to the eastern end of the lake to see the

Sign at the dock at Jellyfish Lake outlines proper tourist behavior while visting.

76

New dock at Jellyfish Lake makes arrivals and departures of the many visitors a safe and easy process.

dispersed more on the northwestern side in the afternoon than on the eastern side in the morning. I began to feel a sting around my neck, but remained in the lake because the lighting was just right for photographs. Jellyfish Lake is not for everybody. Reactions to your first visit vary from awesome, spiritual, cosmic and unbelievable to creepy, fearful, uncomfortable and scary. Some quickly leave, others linger for a long time in this strange new world.

Diving in Jellyfish Lake is both spectacular and eerie. (It is a long trek into the lake with tanks! Researchers and film crews must have a permit to dive in the lakes.) Visitors can explore deeper and stay longer to investigate the communities along the edge. Deep within the lake, jellyfish still completely surrounded you. The sun above orientates you as you gaze at the silhouettes of thousands of jellyfish. Slowly the light dims as you descend into a dark layer of purple bacteria, *Chromatium* sp. Your depth gauge reads about 15-meters at this red bacterial layer that

jellyfish. I swam outside the swarm and saw a distinct boundary between the jellyfish aggregation and the clear morning water. An opening to the sea is at the eastern end of the lake. We saw and felt the water moving from this tunnel during the low tides. Swimming along the edges, I saw the white sea anemones, *Entacmaea medusivora*, attached to fallen branches and protruding mangrove roots. As the day progressed we followed the jellyfish across the lake to the western end. By late afternoon millions of jellyfish gathered at the northwestern end. The aggregation

Path through the jungle to Jellyfish Lake. It's a steep climb but worth it.

is 1 to 2 meters thick. This layer marks the interface between the upper layer of oxygenated (oxic), nutrient poor, turbid water and the lower layer of non-oxygenated (anoxic), clear, dark water below. You do not stay long below the bacteria layer because the waters are highly sulfuric (hydrogen sulfide). The sulfuric waters can cause harm to your body. Hydrogen sulphide can be absored through your skin. This changes the hemoglobin of the blood and prevents it from carrying oxygen. High concentrations of ammonia, phosphate, silica and organic matter are in the bottom water layer. Bottom sediment is composed of plant remnants from mangrove trees living immediately adjacent to the water and jungle vegetation on the steep limestone cliffs encircling the lake.

The jellyfish *Mastigias* sp. and *Aurelia sp.* are the most famous inhabitants of Jellyfish Lake. Yet many organisms make the lake their home. Striped silversides, two species of goby fishes and the big eyed cardinal fish, *Sphaeramia orbicularis* thrive in the lakes. Colonies of white anemone, *Entacmaea medusivora* (formerly *Aiptasia pulchella*) dot the lake's edge. Clusters of black mytilid mussels, other mollusks, several starfish and a vast array of sponges and tunicates live here. Millions of copepods, *Oithona oculata* and *Acrocalanus inermis* (microscopic crustaceans) are food for the moon jellyfish *Aurelia sp.* and the silverside fish. Dr. Laura Martin has studied the ecological relationships between the copepods and jellyfish for several years. The pied cormorant, *Phalacrocorax melanoleucos (deroech)* occasionally fly in the sky above. Even crocodiles live in Jellyfish Lake.

The connections between a lake and the sea determine its chemistry and biology. Completely enclosed deep lakes

Photo by Kevin Davidson

Non-stinging jellyfish.

may have a chemically distinct upper and lower water layer. Shallower lakes are unstratified. When predators cannot enter or survive in the lakes, organisms like jellyfish can successfully grow, reproduce and multiply into large populations. Semi-enclosed lakes may have entrances too narrow to swim or wide enough for a boat to enter. Lake *Ketau* at *Eil Malk* Island is the largest lake in Palau at about 2000-meters long, 350-meters wide and 60-meters deep. There are three Rock Islands within it. Fully grown grey sharks live in *Ketau* Lake and it has well developed mangroves. There are tunnels into Lake *Ketau*, allowing organisms to move between the lake and outer lagoon.

You do not have to go far to enjoy Palau's marine lakes. In June 1994 our guide Mr. Bena Sakuma led us on a wonderful boat tour among the Rock Islands for two days. We meandered around *Ngermeangel* Island one day and *Ngeruktabel* Island the next day. This tour was part of a workshop for local dive and tour guides. Mr. Sakuma was hesitant at first to show us some of the lakes. *If I show you these lakes, what will happen to them in the end?* We explored semi-enclosed lakes and inland marine lakes. While exploring *Ngeruktabel* Island, we visited a lake that

Photo by Kevin Davidson

Photo at left:
Visitors to Jellyfish Lake will find
thousands of these beautiful jellyfish.

Coral Reef Research Foundation

Large goby-like fish found in
Goby Lake. The name of the lake
is not its official name, but one
given it by the photographer.

is only accessible during high tide. To enter you must swim through a dark tunnel about thirty meters long with only the sunlight at the other end to light your way. Stinging feather shaped branches of hydroids wave

chanos (mesekelat) dwell here. Swamp Lake has murky water and mussels, orange sponges and river snappers. Shrimp Lake has millions of transparent shrimp and a large population of the upside-down jellyfish, *Cassiopea* sp.

The next day, we traveled around *Ngermeangel* Island. The highlight of my day was a visit to an enclosed lake less than a five-minute hike into the forest. Low-lying branches touched the water's edge. The branches filtered the sun's rays and brought out iridescent pigments in the coral polyps and scarlet red tunicates. I came back full of a sense of wonderment. There are several lakes at *Ngermeuangel* Island including Big Jellyfish Lake, Goby Lake, Flatworm Lake and two smaller lakes. Big Jellyfish Lake *(Uet ra Edead)* is the largest lake on the island and

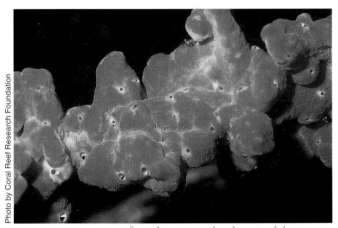

Photo by Coral Reef Research Foundation

Orange sponge found in many inland marine lakes.

Photo by Coral Reef Research Foundation

Delicate tube worm surrounded by sponge.

along the sides and bottom of the tunnel. The tunnel opens up to a deep lake that is full of large coral heads and fish. One semi-enclosed lake had an entrance large enough for our boat to enter during high tide. The mangrove tree *Rhizophora mucronata (tebechel)* lines the lake edge. The seagrass *Enhalus acoroides* carpeted the sandy bottom. The upside-down jellyfish *Cassiopea* sp. pulsated in the blue green water.

The Island of *Ngeruktabel* has several lakes we did not visit that day including "T"- Lake, Swamp Lake and Shrimp Lake. "T" Lake has murky water and banks covered with the grape like algae, *Caulerpa* sp. An unusual sea cucumber covered with long spikes lives here. Small goby fishes, sponges, a school of black surgeonfish, *Acanthurus* sp. and the large silvery milkfish, *Chanos*

has the largest population of the jellyfish *Mastigias* sp. in Palau. Big Jellyfish Lake has the river snapper *Lutjanus argentimaculatus (kedesau 'l iengel)* and orange and black *tunicates.* (I describe my experience in this lake during a kayak trip with Ethan Daniels. Please refer to Chapter 6 on Canoes, Rafts and Kayaks.) Goby Lake *(Uet ra Utoi)* has a small population of the *Mastigias* jellyfish and five species of goby fish. One type of goby-like fish (actually an *Eleotrid* fish) called *Ophiocara porocephala* is over twelve inches long! Flatworm Lake is named after its most abundant inhabitants–flatworms. Two smaller lakes connect by a tunnel with large caves along their banks. The tunnel floor has noxious stinging sponges. Scientists continue to unravel the mysteries of these lakes.

A smaller Rock Island called *Ongael* has a lake with

thousands of marine snails as well as algae, sponges and gobies. *Kaibakku* Lake lies within a Rock Island in Iwayama Bay. Access by land is difficult because the incline is very steep. There is a tunnel about 10 meters underwater and 100 meters long that leads into the lake. Within the tunnel are brittle stars, sponges, ascidians and spider crabs. These are just a few highlights discovered by scientists and visitors in some of the many marine lakes of Palau.

It is common to see up to twelve tour boats at Jellyfish Lake in a day. As many as 30,000 tourists visit this lake every year. The Palau Government asked Dr. Bill Hamner to compare current biological conditions (1993) of Jellyfish Lake with conditions before it became a tourist attraction (1981). He found that the numbers of jellyfish and overall chemistry of the lake were unchanged. However, he found that the layer of fine sediments decreased within the small channel entering the lake. Dr. Hamner did not find evidence that either the jellyfish or stratification of the lake were adversely affected by tourist traffic. Today, a floating dock allows tourists to enter the deeper end of the lake without disturbing the sediments.

In 1995 I led a group of college students to the lake. We observed broken mangrove roots, especially at points where the channel narrows. Within the lake, we counted the number of injured jellyfish as we swam to and from the dense aggregations. We counted an average of six injured jellyfish per person. We

Mussel shells encrusted with orange sponge.

Photo by Coral Reef Research Foundation

observed jellyfish pushed and disturbed by each kick of our fins. (Kicking with your feet or fins creates air bubbles that get caught underneath the jellyfish. The bubbles create extra buoyancy causing the jellyfish to rise to the surface. When this happens, I gently dislodge the bubbles from under the jellyfish so it can descend.)

The students made several recommendations to Koror State government to help minimize the damaging impact to Jellyfish Lake. They suggested a safer docking area and hand railings for the steep slope areas. The students suggested a mangrove boardwalk and floating ramp to eliminate swimming fins. They recommended limiting the number of visitors into the lake each day. The students recommended a concrete walkway with handrails on either side to limit the area of impact to the island's forests. A mangrove board-walk along the channel's edge enables tour guides to educate guests about the unique mangrove ecosystem and the oriental mangrove, *Bruguiera gymnorhiza (denges)*.

During 1998 Koror State and the Palau Conservation Society completed an improvement project for *Ongeim'l Tketau Uet*. (The U.S. Department

Common pink sponge.

Photo by Coral Reef Research Foundation

Photo by Coral Reef Research Foundation

Jellyfish-eating anemone found in Jellyfish Lake.

Photo by Coral Reef Research Foundation

Mangrove Snapper.

of Interior and RARE Center for Tropical Conservation funded this improvement project.) I went to visit in June of 1998. Wooden floating docks are at the beginning of the trail where boats drop off passengers and at the entry point into Jellyfish Lake. Educational boards and permanent markers describe the unique ecosystem of the Lake and surrounding forest. Trees labeled along the trail include *Guettarda speciosa (blau)* with its large straight elephant skin trunk and the poison tree *Semecarpus venenosus (tonget)*. *Pandanus aimiriikensis (chertochet)* and *Horsfieldia palauensis (chersachel)* have labels. Sections of steep trail are graded and have rope handrails. The trail circumvents the mangroves. Visitors snorkel in deeper water rather than the shallow mangrove channel and

disturb less sediment in the lake. Guests enjoy a safe and educational visit. There is even a compost toilet by the entrance of the trail. Koror State has laws to manage and restrict access to *Ongeim'l Tketau Uet*. Permit fees help finance the management of this truly unique ecosystem.

In late 1998 the *Mastigias* sp. jellyfish disappeared in Jellyfish Lake. Today the lake is again filled with millions of jellyfish. Several factors may have caused this disappearance including climate changes and tourist impact. All of Palau's marine lakes need protection. As we continue to discover and enjoy the lakes, Bena's question still lingers in my mind. *If I show you these lakes, what will happen to them in the end?*

REFERENCES

Colin P. L. and C. Arneson. 1995. *Tropical Pacific Invertebrates.* The Coral Reef Research Foundation.

Hamner W. M. and I. R. Hauri. 1981. *Long-distance horizontal migrations of zooplankton* (Scyphomedusae: *Mastigias.*) Limnol. Oceanogr. 26(3) pp. 414-423.

Hamner W. M., R. W. Gilmer and P.P. Hamner. 1982. *The physical, chemical, and biological characteristics of a stratified, saline, sulfide lake in Palau. Limnol.* Oceanogr., 27(5) 896-909.

Hamner, W. M. 1994. *Current Biological Status (1994) of Jellyfish Lake, Macharchar.* Prepared for Division of Marine Resources, Republic of Palau.

Hamner W. M. and P. P. Hamner. 1998. *Stratified Marine Lakes of Palau (Western Caroline Islands).* Physical Geography. 19.3, pp. 175-220.

Sharron, L. 1995. *Marine Lakes of Palau.* Vol 1. No 3. Pacific Below. Marine Images.

Conversations and information shared with Dr. Pat Colin, Lori Colin and Dr. Laura Martin and Dr. Michael Dawson.

Canoes, Rafts and Kayaks

Palauans are seafaring people. The first settlers sailed by canoe to Palau from other regions. Canoes were a common sight in the lagoon waters. Palauan canoes were unique in the Pacific, because they floated low in the water and were shallow compared to the length and size of the boat. Paddles and sails propel these small, light, keel-less boats. Palauans used several types of canoes. Sailing canoes called *"kaeb"* were used for racing and sending messages. A smaller sailing and paddling canoe *(kotraol)* was used for fishing and cargo. Battles between rival clans were fought using the war canoe called *"kabekl."* Cargo canoes *(borotong)* transported goods from place to place. Early immigrants arrived in ocean sailing canoes.

The Southwest Islands had their own type of canoe called *"mlai a bul."* The Southwest islanders were skilled navigators. Eventually most Palauans lost the navigation skills that were vital for long distance navigation. Perhaps the relative closeness of the main Palauan islands made long sea voyages unnecessary. Maybe the new settlers were content with the beautiful islands they discovered.

Sailing canoes had a mast and one triangular sail, an outrigger with a raised platform and a rudder that was not permanently attached to the canoe. The raised platform on the outrigger was usually occupied by the captain. The mast is positioned essentially in the middle of the canoe, half way between bow and stern and held upright by a coconut fiber rope attached at the top of the mast and anchored to the outermost rail of the outrigger. The woven *pandanas* sail is attached to a wooden boom at the bottom and has a rigid wooden spar lashed to its leading edge. When sailing, the bottom tip of the wooden spar on the leading edge of the sail is temporarily tied to the forward most point of the canoe so that a large portion of the sail is in front of the mast. This configuration produces speed. The canoe is always sailed with the outrigger to windward. To reverse direction one need only release the tip of the wooden spar on the leading edge of the sail, transport it to the other end of the canoe and tie it. The helmsman takes his rudder paddle to the opposite end of the boat. The bow now becomes the stern and off you go. Each type of canoe had unique features. The large racing canoes *(kaeb)* were thirty-three feet long. Palauans decorated their canoes with small wooden statutes of the

Photo at right.
Palauan sailing canoe, *borotong*, was used to transport people and cargo and could be propelled by either sail or paddle. Canoes only approached a village with its outrigger facing the sea as it was considered impolite to do otherwise.

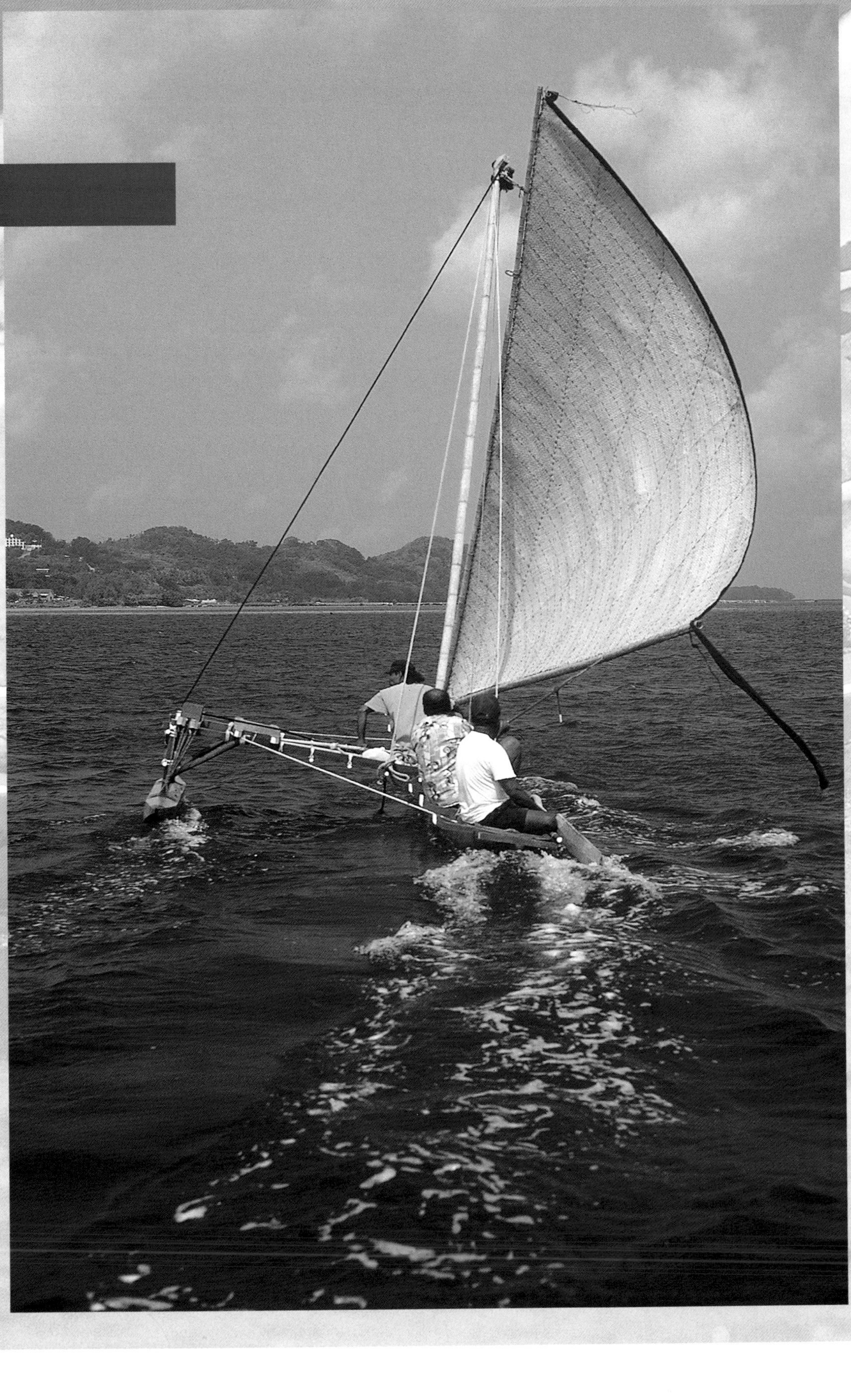

The *borotong* was a shallow draft vessel that could easily navigate the shallow waters of the reef. Palauan canoes rarely ventured outside the reefs.

were attached to the canoe by "Y" shaped pieces of mangrove wood. The war canoe had a double wooden beam with several supports for the outrigger. Canoe paddles had bulging tips that made a whistling sound with each stroke. Palauans carved more detail on the steering paddle than on the paddles used for rowing. The steering paddle had a pointed end and was located at the back of the canoe.

Skilled craftsmen *(dachelbai)* could build canoes in about one and a half years. Payment was one Palauan money bead *(chebucheb)* that was blue with white dots. The hull of the canoe was hewn from a single tree. The hardwood tree *Serianthes kanehirae (ukall)* was the preferred tree because it was strong and a good carving wood. Palauans used the breadfruit tree *Artocarpus altilis (meduu)* and the large tree *Calophyllum inophyllum (btaches)* to make canoes as well. The master carver and his assistants went to the forest to

kingfisher bird on the stern and bow. White egg cowerie shells, *Ovula ovum,* hung along the sides.

The smaller sailing canoes *(kotraol)* were ten to thirty-five feet long. Old photographs of these canoes show decorations of six small crosses with inlaid clamshell. White egg cowrie shells decorated the sides of the boat. Canoes had sails made from *Pandanus* leaves *(cheludel).* The people of Peleliu and *Ngarchelong* were renown for their sail making skills.

The war canoe *(kabekl)* was the largest canoe reaching lengths of fifty feet. They were elaborately decorated. Palauans meticulously attached eighty to one hundred egg cowrie shells on the loose board across the outrigger. They carved faces on the ends of the thwart bars. Outriggers

Palauan war caone. Almost 50 ft. (15 meters) long. The Palauan name is "kabekl."

select the right tree. The trees had to be large in size and facing a certain direction. There was a spiritual aspect to building canoes. Once the master craftsman selected a tree, his team of men burned the bottom of the trunk. The burning caused the leaves to drop. They cut the tree and removed the branches. They made their first rough carving of the shape of the canoe at the site where the tree fell. Their work required about two months. They then brought the rough shaped canoe to the canoe house (diangel) to do the remaining work.

The true mark of an established men's club in a village was the possession of a war canoe. Elaborate war canoes were essential during power struggles between villages. Each village kept several war canoes in the canoe house. War canoes were a village show-case for ceremonial events. Palauans adorned the bow and stern with a variety of shells strung on a cord. Builders de-signed the war canoe to rise high out of the water. The smallest war

Canoe being constructed in 1993 at Senior Citizens Center in Koror. The knowledge and tradition is passed on from generation to generation.

canoes held four to five people. The largest war canoes carried about thirty-seven people. The chief sat in the middle of the canoe. An elder sat on the platform in-structing the paddlers. During battle, two warriors sat in a ready position on bamboo poles placed under the outrigger. Sailors achieved great skills in manuevering their canoes whether by sail or paddle. During a ceremo-nial visit, Palauans paddled their canoes in formation. Their rhythmic paddling caused the canoe to glide gracefully across the water. During the Micronesian Games of 1998 we witnessed these skills once again.

In Palauan custom, one does not use an item made by their own hands. Chiefs purchased canoes built by a master craftsman (dachelbai) from another village. A man kept his canoe in good condition but paid a master craftsman to construct it. This practice resulted in the continuous flow of goods throughout the village. Canoe construction kept communities productive and ensured the transfer of Palauan money.

They used fruit of the tree *Paranari glaberrimum* (cheritem) to obtain a red colored oil. They scraped and boiled the fruit to extract its reddish oil. They painted the canoe with red clay pigment and then coated it with the reddish oil extract. They applied the red clay and oil several times. Craftsmen used red and white paints derived from clay minerals to decorate the canoe. They used yellow paints derived from the ginger plant to color the inside of the canoe. They soaked the bark of man-grove tree *Rhizophora mucronata* (tebechel) to make a maroon brown colored paint as well. Once painted, they rubbed the canoe with coconut oil, then rubbed and polished it with dry coconut husk. Finally, they decorated the canoe with inlaid shells. They placed the shell inlays along the outside of the canoe.

Palauans carved miniature canoes as vehicles for spirits and souls. When a high chief became sick, a skilled craftsman carved and decorated a small boat to carry the spirit of a deity to the village. The deity healed the sick. Priests protected an entire community by placing the small canoe, about two meters long, in the men's house

(bai). The *Tobi* islanders had a spirit house dedicated to their high god. Inside the house, a spirit ship served to hold and carry the deity. The islanders placed offerings

engine. Soon many families purchased motor boats and the number of canoes became less and less.

Palauans pass the skills of canoe building down through the generations. Today the few remaining canoe builders of Palau construct traditional canoes upon special request. In 1982 *Ngchesar* State built a war canoe that they display at their village canoe house *(diangel).* In 1992 *Airai* master canoe builder Ilapsis Edeluchel built two traditional sailing canoes through a project funded

Palauan kids spend an afternoon fishing and exploring the inland waterways. The *"brer"* is easily propelled with the use of a long bamboo pole.

Bamboo rafts, called *"brer,"* in the mangroves are a common sight on *Babeldaob* today.

inside the ship and the chiefs had yearly feasts to honor the ship. A painting of the frigate bird sitting on top of a crescent moon decorated the end of this special canoe.

One day I asked my mother-in-law, Ngemelas, now 86 years old, about the early days of canoes. She recalled her childhood days when her father had a *"kaeb"* and they sailed out in the open sea. Ngemelas's father also owned a *"kotraol"* that they used for fishing and transportation. She said this was their main means of travel throughout her childhood. The Japanese introduced motorized boats in Palau. During the Japanese era Ngemelas's father purchased his first motor boat with a 6-horsepower

by the State Unit Agency on Aging and the Senior Citizen Center in Koror. One of the canoes was displayed at the airport where it was admired by visitors. Shortly thereafter it was donated to Mie Prefecture in Japan by President Nakamura. President Nakamura donated it to

Japanese students. Mandy Etpison commissioned a canoe master craftsman to build another sailing canoe. It is refreshing to see traditional canoes constructed. Perhaps we will see traditional canoes in the lagoons once again?

Palauans use at least three types of simple rafts *(brer)*. Fisherfolk make rafts of six bamboo poles to hold light loads like *Trochus* shell *(semum)* during the harvest season. Some have personal rafts made of seven or eight pieces of bamboo. Some personal rafts have a small seat called a *"bluu."* They make the seat with bamboo and other types of wood. The third and largest type of raft is called a *"cholechutel."* It consists of ten or more bamboo poles and serves as a cargo raft to carry large pieces of wood and rock. The *"cholechutel"* is usually a community raft. The most common raft is the personal bamboo raft *(brer)*. Men and women still use the bamboo raft to fish and carry large loads. Today rafts are less common because motorized boats can do similar tasks.

A bamboo raft is easy to construct. A raft is simply made with several pieces of bamboo cut to size and lashed together. Fishermen use these rafts to set their nets and fish traps out on the reef. Women take rafts to the mangrove edge to collect clams and to the fringing reef to harvest fish and sea cucumbers. Women usually take along young boys or girls who pole the raft through the water using a long bamboo pole called a *"dekel."* The women sit and help balance as their children learn the art of poling. To pole a long distance is a tough job. Often the poling distance is short; out the mangrove channel *(taoch)* or to the edge of the fringing reef. I have happy memories of poling with friends through the mangrove

channels. When my husband and I were first married, we stayed at a small house at *Ngeruluobel* near the canoe house. We made a bamboo raft and poled it through the mangrove channel and onto the fringing reef. We went far enough to catch a few fish.

During the 1950's islanders began to use tin to make their canoes. Americans introduced corrugated tin to the islands. Inventive young boys made canoes by simply folding the tin in half and tapering the ends. The tin canoe was easier to make than a bamboo raft. In the 1970's, children played in the shallow lagoon in home-made tin canoes. Today tin canoes are rare. I did see a

The end of an era as the outboard motor overtakes the bamboo pole as the most widely used means of water propulsion.

Tin canoes are quickly constructed with a sheet of corrugated roofing tin.
Good balance is essential and paddling an art in these most sensitive of crafts.

group of boys have a great time with a tin canoe in *Ngarchelong* in 1997.

Within the past twenty years, fiberglass canoes have become popular. One spring afternoon in 1990 my husband and I were going to *Airai* Bay to observe fishermen attempting to catch rabbitfish, *Siganus fuscescens (meas)* at their spawning grounds. Our boat was having engine problems, so we decided to use an available fiberglass canoe. We went along *Airai's* Rock Islands and through the *Chongelungel* Channel. We paddled against the channel's strong outgoing currents. Clarence paddled in the back to provide the extra strength through the channel. Once past the channel, we glided into the calm bay. We joined other fishermen at the spawning grounds. There were a few boats, canoes and bamboo rafts. A few

usual quick ride by speedboat.

A welcome change to the fast pace of speedboats is the kayak. The kayak takes you back to a time of self-reliance and a slower pace. At first, many laughed at these "toy canoes," made of plastic and bright crayon colors. Within a few years, kayaks became popular as Palauans discovered that kayaking is simple fun for all ages. The kayak is lighter and easier to manage than a tin canoe, bamboo raft or fiberglass canoe. One person can launch and maneuver it easily. It has no sharp edges and is hard to sink. Some areas are easier to access by kayak. A common kayak route goes around *Ngermeangel, Ngeruktabel* and *Ulebsechel* Islands and *Airai's* Rock Islands. The kayak moves quietly through the water without causing a disturbance. Narrow passages teem with colorful soft and

Kayaks quickly became popular in Palau as an environmentally friendly means of water transportation and method of exploration for tourists.

men teased younger men casting nets for the first time. Most men were silent and intent on their catch. As each man caught his share, he joined the other boats to share the excitement of the day. As the sun set we headed back across the bay. I remember the canoe ride more than the fishing. While paddling, I observed each island closely as we slowly passed. It was a peaceful ride compared to the

hard corals and sponges that feed on particles that pass with the swift currents. You can paddle alone and find solitude in secluded spots.

Kayaking brings back childhood memories of tin canoes and traditional canoes. I visualize a past generation paddling from village to village. Lisa King introduced me to kayaking in 1995. I admit I thought it would be too

much work. She told me not to worry because we would stay within the inner Rock Islands of Nikko Bay (Iwayama Bay). I met her at *Ngermid* and we carried the two kayaks down to the water. The kayaks were light and easy to handle.

She gave me some simple instructions about paddling. Before I knew it, I was meandering around the coves and Rock Islands. We snorkeled along the reef edge where we saw beautiful whorled plates of coral. We had a great deal of fun. Our voices seemed loud as we glided through the quiet lagoon. Lisa went kayaking whenever she had free time. I could understand now why she wanted to share the experience of kayaking with me. Her eyes lit up as she explained how she hoped kayaking would become a successful venture in Palau.

Well, Lisa's beginning efforts and enthusiasm did just that. Now there are four kayaking operations in Palau: Palau Kayak Tours, operating through Fish and Fins;

Planet Blue, operating through Sam's Dive Tours, which began kayaking tours in 1996; *Uel* Tours and IMPAC Kayak Tours. You can kayak many places. Larger speedboats will tow the kayaks up to rivers in *Babeldaob* or south to *Ulong* Island. You can enjoy a river ride or meander through the Rock Islands.

Palauan kids enjoy an afternoon of paddling.

The most efficient means of getting from place to place.

Two years after I first went kayaking with Lisa, I went kayaking again. In July 1997 I went with Ethan Daniels, a kayak guide working with Planet Blue. Mr. Ron Leidich planned and choreographed the tours and trained Ethan. We had a choice of three alternative routes for the day. We choose to go up to Big Jellyfish Lake, Koror and through several other lakes around *Ngermeuangel* Island. Once we chose our tour,

Ethan briefed us about kayaks and how to use them. Then the men loaded the two seated kayaks onto a long speedboat.

The speedboat dropped us at our first destination: Big Jellyfish Lake or *"Wet ra Edead"* on *Ngermeuangel* Island.

89

A PERSONAL TOUR OF PALAU · CHAPTER 6: CANOES, RAFTS AND KAYAKS

We anchored our kayaks near shore and prepared our-selves for the twenty-minute hike to the lake. A large fruitbat flew high over the Rock Island. We scrambled over steep limestone terrain. The static-like songs of the cicada serenaded us. Vibrations of special abdominal membranes made of chitin produce the cicadas' songs. While climbing, we watched out for the "poison tree" *Semecarpus venenosus (tonget)* with its telltale black sap oozing from its trunk. We saw four poison trees along the path — just where you wanted to hold on to something. We stopped midway to examine some calcium calcite. Yapese made their money from this crystalline rock long ago. The people of Yap would sail to Palau to quarry large pieces of calcium calcite cutting and shaping it into a circle with a hole in the center. Men carried the money using a wooden pole that passed through the hole in the center. Yapese used early tools of clamshell, so the work to carve one stone money was enormous.

Then, there was the lake. As we came closer, we saw thousands of jellyfish, *Mastigias* sp., on the water's

marine biologists in our group built a raft for their research in the lake. We used their stationary raft to carefully slide into the lake without disturbing the delicate communities of sponges, tunicates and mussels along the edges. The jellyfish ranged in size from a thumbnail to a closed fist. As I swam into the lake I became part of a giant bowl of cream jellyfish in clear blue soup. Jellyfish lakes are unique to Palau. Each visit to a jellyfish lake is different. The time, lighting and sensa-tion of being in and among them is never the same. I only saw two white moon jellies, *Aurelia* sp., in the deeper water compared to the abundant golden jellyfish, *Mastigias* sp. My eyes gazed at the jellyfish for a while. Then my curiosity drew me to the edge of the lakes.

The benthic communities were like an exotic painting brushed around the rim of the lake. Splashes of brilliant yellow, orange, lavender, soft pink and burgundy sponges blended with thousands of golden tunicates tightly packed into every free space. Patches of delicate green algae interrupted the seascape. Dozens of small mottled

Southwest Island girls practice launching of canoe during Youth Day race competition held in Koror.

surface. At the edge of the lake, there was a small stand of mangrove trees, *Bruguiera gymnorhiza (denges)*. Two

sea cucumbers were feeding within the algal mats. At least two species of mussels were jammed on every mangrove

root lining the lake. Mussels coated with white chocolate sponges tempted my taste buds. I swam in wonderment, closely taking in everything I could. Suddenly I saw six large river snappers, *Lutjanus argentimaculatus (kedesau 'l iengel)* approaching me. They came so close. It seemed as if the snappers came to greet me. Perhaps they were curious to see this strange large visitor. It was still and quiet in the lake: no waves and no wind. Several species of fish including gobies and cardinalfish were present. I looked up and saw my companions waiting for me by the raft where we had entered. As we headed out, I knew that I would be back.

My thoughts still in the lake, I hardly noticed some land crabs scurrying for cover. A blue tailed skink paused and then ran away. We heard the distant call of the Palauan fruit dove, *Ptilinopus pelewensis (biib)* and an Eclectus parrot, *Eclectus nonatus (iakkotsiang)* overhead.

Small dugout canoes such as this one are light and relatively fast. Many are made from breadfruit trees which have soft wood and are easy to carve.

Now, it was time to paddle. My kayak entry was not graceful, but I quickly got the rhythm of the paddle strokes. Ethan paddled in the back, graciously compensating for my inexperience. We kayaked to Tarzan cave. I had passed this cave many times but never took notice. At the entrance, fragments of ancient clay pottery were cemented into the white beach rock. A small swiftlet, *Aerodramus vanikorensis (chesisekiaid)*, was nesting in a hole in the cave's ceiling by the inner entrance. It is the only bird in Palau that can use sound rather than sight to "echo locate" its way and find food. Stalactites and stalagmites hung down throughout the cave. Stalactites

are icicle-shaped calcium deposits that hang from the ceiling or side of a cave. The stalactites slowly dripped liquid calcium, drop by drop. These drops eventually will form upward columns called stalagmites that form on the floor of the cave and resemble inverted stalactites. It is important not to touch the stalagmites and stalactites. The oil on our hands can block the openings from which the carbon water drips and prevent the formation of the icicles of calcium.

Within the cave was a collapsed ceiling. I took a closer look and saw Japanese symbols etched on the rock. Japanese soldiers had spent time in these caves during World War II. There were imitative or "fake" Japanese characters scribbled nearby by some local graffiti artists. The center of the cave was open to the sky. Sun beams reflected off the green vegetation and long vines that dangled freely downward. However, one very long and thick root grew straight down to the ground where we stood. More roots sprung from the main root and sprawled like snakes along the cave floor. I did not know what tree could have such a long root system, except perhaps the fig tree, *Ficus* sp. *(lulk)*. We directed our flashlights into a dark compartment of the cave and saw small delicate crystal columns forming from the low ceiling. We saw the curtain formations of fused columns. Then we flashed our light on several human bones: a skull, some leg bones and even a tooth. It is thought that the bones are not Palauan. Since the discovery of these bones, Palau's Division of Cultural Affairs designated this area as a preservation site.

Small outrigger canoe found on the beach on *Sonsorol* Island in the Southwest Islands of Palau. This canoe is used daily for fishing along the reefs edge. Southwest islanders call this canoe *"mlai a bul."*

We went into another deeper and darker cave where we saw more Japanese symbols. This time it was a Japanese woman's name. We imagined lonely Japanese soldiers thinking of home. Within the dark and deep cave, our lights flashed upon large fat crickets clinging to the cave walls. These large crickets are blind and did not respond to the flashlight. Their extra long antennae pick up small vibrations nearby. Their predator, a scorpion-like spider, lives among them. Ethan showed us a spider embedded in an amber plastic mold so we could easily examine its structure. Scorpion-like spiders can see in the dark and feed on the crickets. If you touch a cricket's antennae, it leaps out towards you. The low entrance could give a nice bump to the head if you tried to leave too quickly in the dark. A light rain shower was just ending as we were ready to move onward. We waited a bit, examining the mollusks that had formed pits around the undercut of the Rock Island. We found a brittle starfish in a small pool.

Delicate shallow pools were forming around the stalagmites.

If you look closely in the top branches you will find the Collared Kingfisher, called *"tengadidik"* by Palauans. These birds are commonly found along the waters edge and can be approached quietly with the help of a canoe.

When the rain stopped, we kayaked through the only strong currents of our tour. These currents came from the tides flowing out from the east entrance of Iwayama Bay. We headed in, just past Lee Marvin's beach (named after the famous actor who did a film called "Hell in the Pacific" on this beach in the 1960's). We rode the waves into Blacktip Shark Lake. This lake had a wide entrance. We headed towards an opening formed after two Rock Islands had fused together. The water was very shallow, yet we were able to glide effortlessly throughout the lake.

Canoe paddling competition has become very popular in Palau. Paddling teams are made up of women or men and often both.

We saw two young blacktip sharks, about two feet long, slowly cruise by. Ethan stood up in the kayak, looking over the water, to scout for his favorite sharks. We saw a few squid and some mullets. We did not get out of our kayaks. We just glided along.

Birds were abundant in this lake. A couple of noisy fantail birds, *Rhipidura lepida (melimdelebteb)* chased each other among the low branches hanging over the lake. A reef heron, *Egretta sacra (sechou)* and a Rufous night heron, *Nycticorax caledonicus (melabaob)* flew over head as did the tropic bird. We saw the red flashes of several honeyeaters, *Myzomela rubratra kobayahii (chesisebangiau)*. We watched as the collared kingfisher, *Todirhamphus chloris teraokai (tengadidik)* dove underwater to feed. It was a peaceful place. As we left, I noted

another type of mangrove tree, *Sonneratia alba (urur)* growing along the edge of the lake. Mangrove trees seem to grow well within these sheltered lakes. No other boat was in this lake, only kayaks could navigate in these shallow waters.

We went around the point of the Rock Island to a small beach exposed during the low tide. We sat on the soft white sand and ate lunch. Ethan explained how dependent our tour was upon the tides. We had been moving with the tides rather than against them. There was only a limited time where we could enter Blacktip Shark Lake and other areas along the way. Many beaches and reefs lay exposed during the lowest tides of the year in late spring and summer. We looked at a map to see where we had been and where we were heading. It felt good to know where we were. A kayaker can be easily confused while navigating among the many Rock Islands of Palau. After lunch we kayaked around the point of the Rock Island and along the south end of *Malakal* Harbor. On our way we saw a small green turtle. The turtle poked its head above water at least six times, which is unusual. Turtles usually dive under and emerge only once at a distance. As we entered another lake, a motor boat with three Palauan men was just leaving. They were probably looking for sardines for bait. It is common to find sardines in these more accessible lakes. Within the lake we saw a wreck of a small cargo ship that sunk during the war. Our guide recalled events that occurred in Palau during WWII. We were a bit somber thinking of the impact the war had on the Islands. The wrecks scattered throughout Palau are a constant reminder of the past.

We headed for our last destination: Mandarinfish Lake. As we approached, a large tourist boat was just leaving. Their engines broke the silence and our guide was visibly disappointed. He explained he did not like large boats in these areas, because they might disturb the fragile systems

The Sydney 2000 Olympic Torch, shown here in the Rock Islands. Part of its journey through Palau was made on a series of canoes paddled by Palauan crew members.

within the lakes. Mandarinfish Lake, as Blacktip Shark Lake, is not semi-enclosed like the Big Jellyfish Lake. We just kayaked into them. There was a strong current at the mouth of this lake, as it had a narrower entrance than Blacktip Shark Lake. A cluster of beautiful pink fan corals lined the shaded edges of the entrance. Fan corals grow perpendicular to the currents in order to catch plankton as it passes. At the far end of the lake, there is a rush of water that sounds like a waterfall. This water is draining out from another lake that connects to Mandarinfish Lake. The lake is just a five-minute walk over a small ridge. We did not go into the lake over the ridge, instead we anchored our kayaks and swam towards a large head of *Porites* coral to see the mandarinfish.

The coral head was over two meters high and four meters wide. As we swam around the coral head I spotted four mandarinfish tucked between the branch tips. The

mandarinfish is a splendid little dragonet, *Synchiropus splendidus.* It has a psychedelic pattern of green, blue, orange and yellow colors, unmatched by any of its kind. Hundreds of the blue-eyed apogonid, *Apogon leptacanthus,* a few dozen black belted cardinalfish, *Archamia zosterophora* and the large Pajama cardinalfish, *Sphaeramia nematoptera,* hovered more conspicuously over the large coral head. One slingjaw wrasse, *Epibulus insidiator* passed by. The colorful eight banded butterflyfish, *Chaetodon octofasciatus* and the latticed butterflyfish, *Chaetodon raffelsii* wove between the coral branches. As we wandered across the lake, we saw a large school of parrotfish. The school included the juvenile humphead parrotfish, *Bolbometopon muricatum (berdebed)*, Bleeker's parrotfish, *Scarus bleekeri (mellemau),* Pacific longnose parrotfish, *Hipposcarus longiceps (ngyoach)* and the black, green and purple color phases of the bullethead

parrotfish, *Scarus sordidus (mellemau)*. The herd of parrotfish swam away over the coral substrate in a tight pack that dispersed as we approached them. Six lined or yellow spotted rabbitfish, *Siganus lineatus (klsebuul)* passed by. The edges of the lake had iridescent corals that grew well in the shade provided by the overhanging forest. Slowly we came back to our kayaks and awaited our pick up boat.

Our guide hoisted the kayaks onto the deck of the boat. We sat between the kayaks and held them as we zoomed back at full speed across *Malakal* Harbor. The boat hit the wake of a passing dive boat, so we got one last splash. All day, we had been learning and exploring. Now, we could kayak! We knew more about Palau's geology and the ecology of birds, insects, fish, turtles and sharks. We saw the wreckage of World War II. We explored lakes, caves and beaches. As we sped back, I thought what a wonderful way to spend your last day in Palau.

As I heard the plane fly overhead that night, I wondered what my new friends' lasting thoughts were. As they looked out their dark plane window would their minds still see visions of the turquoise waters enclosed by limestone cliffs? As they drowsed off to sleep, would they dream of the reflection of forests on blue-green waters? Did the calls of fruitbats, terns, honeyeaters, kingfishers, fantails, doves and cockatoos still linger in their ears? Would a flash of crayon colored corals, blacktip sharks, mandarinfish and the amazing Big Jellyfish Lake cross their minds? Did they wonder as I wondered-if we just dreamed or truly sensed the seafarers' past that day together on the lagoon? The quiet timeless lagoon that was now thousands of miles away.

REFERENCES

Conversations with Simeon Adelbai, Ethan Daniels, Mandy Thijssen-Etpison, Lisa King, Ngemelas Kitalong, Ron Leidich and Kempis Mad.

95

Beaches

What is it about a stretch of sand that brings us so much joy? Palau's beaches are found throughout the archipelago offering endless choices for sand lovers. The Southwest Atolls, 200 to 400 miles south of the main archipelago, have beaches with nesting areas for green turtles and terns. *Angaur* Island is a raised coral platform 7 miles southwest of the main archipelago. White beaches punctuate *Angaur's* rugged limestone coastline. Blowholes spew forth fountains of seawater high into the air. Peleliu Island is a raised coral platform that lies within the southern lagoon's barrier reef. Peleliu is 4.6 miles in length and is home to several famous wave-swept beaches. The more isolated Honeymoon Beach lines Peleliu's eastern shore and has an aura of sweet romance. Peleliu's western beaches, Orange and White Beach haunt veterans of World War II. A backdrop of Bloody Nose Ridge reminds us of the human price of victory.

Within the southern lagoon, fine white sands envelop the famous Rock Islands. Over four hundred Rock Islands offer tucked away beaches of solitude and mystery. *Babeldaob*, Palau's largest island, has miles of

beach along its northeastern coast. A sand highway weaves around the shoreline. Abrupt volcanic boulders thrust skyward and seaward, offering a vantage point to gaze out over an expansive fringing reef. White waves crash against the reef's edge with an endless blue ocean beyond. Fifteen miles north of *Babeldaob* lie the beaches of *Kayangel* Atoll, where white sand fades into a gentle blue green lagoon. Each place, each beach, invites you to explore its secrets and immerse yourself in its beauty.

While exploring the beaches you walk among a variety of plants adapted to the hot sun, salt water and wind. Special floating seeds of beach plants travel with the ocean's currents throughout the Pacific region. The beach morning glory, *Ipomoea pes-caprae (kebeaschol, kebeas* = vine and *chol* = beach) carpets the sand, its green succulent leaves punctuated with lavender flowers. Bright yellow flowers of *Wedelia biflora (ngesil)* decorate the beaches. The beach pea, *Vigna marina (keldelel)* with its yellow flower and brown seedpod climbs along the sand. The beach pea shrub, *Sophora tomentosa (dudurs)* has yellow flowers and pods with tightly wrapped seeds. The heliotrope tree, *Tournefortia aregentea (rirs)* has

Photo at right:
The entire west side of *Kayangel* Island, fronting on the lagoon, is a white blaze of sand.

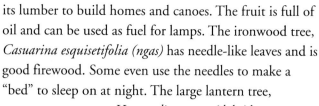

strings of berries that look like caterpillars. Three types of butterflies *(bangikoi)* feed upon its small white flowers and lay eggs in its leaves. The cat's claw tree, *Erythrina variegata* var. *orientalis (roro)* produces large, scarlet red flowers with petals resembling a cat's claw. This striking tree is hard to miss when in bloom.

Palauans live along the beaches and spend the summer months at the Rock Islands. Long ago many Palauans lived along the beach. They depended upon plants for medicine, firewood, lumber and food. The slender vine *Ipomoea littoralis (torech)* with lavender flowers grows over low vegetation. Palauans used the crushed stem and leaves of this vine to heal their wounds. The flowers of the small tree *Pemphis acidula (ngis)* have white wrinkled petals and red fruit. Palauans finely shaved its red bark and wrapped it up in fibers of the coconut palm, *Cocos nucifera (lius).* Then they dipped *ngis* into saltwater and applied it to a sore tooth. The common shrub *Scaevola sericea, (korrai, kirrai* or *raielchol)* has juicy leaves and a unique "half flower" whose five petals are deeply divided. Palauans boil its leaves to make a tea that is used for stomach aches, eye medicine or as a tonic for energy.

The large shade tree *Calophyllum inophyllum (btaches)* has green fruit the size of a golf ball and shiny green leaves. Palauans planted this tree along the shore and used

On the Northeast side of *Babeldaob* from *Ulimang* to *Choll* there is about a three mile stretch of beautiful white sandy beach that in part ends abruptly against volcanic outcroppings and in other places blends in slowly with the shore vegetation.

its lumber to build homes and canoes. The fruit is full of oil and can be used as fuel for lamps. The ironwood tree, *Casuarina esquisetifolia (ngas)* has needle-like leaves and is good firewood. Some even use the needles to make a "bed" to sleep on at night. The large lantern tree, *Hernandia sonora (doko)* has a smooth trunk and lantern shaped white fleshy fruit. Its wood is light and used for firewood.

The coconut palm *Cocos nucifera (lius)* has more uses than any other plant in Palau. There are over thirty Palauan words describing either the stage of growth or the usage of coconuts. Coconut palm logs are split and used as siding for shelters or as planks for benches. The coconut fronds make excellent roofing, baskets and food wrappers for grated tapioca *(bilum),* fish or pork. The

Aerial view of *Angaur* shows its airstrip and rugged coastline. There are also many white sandy beaches between the rocky outcroppings.

Photo by Coral Reef Research Foundation

midribs of the fronds are stripped and bundled together to make brooms *(skobang).* The coconut at its middle growth stage *(mengur)* has sweet juice and soft meat that you can remove with your fingers and eat. Mature coconuts *(metau)* that have fallen to the ground are boiled

to make oil for skin care and cooking. Coconut milk is squeezed from the grated coconut meat and used to enhance fish soup and other foods. The inner meat of a very old coconut has a foam-like texture and makes a sweet tasting snack. Villagers planted many coconut palms on the larger Rock Islands. You see spaced rows of coconut trees from a distance. Coconuts floated to many islands and grew naturally.

Lavender Beach Morning Glories blossom randomly to add color and beauty on many beaches.

Sea turtles play a vital role in Palauan culture and depend upon the beach for survival. Sea turtles are the most threatened animal of the beach. I will explain the sea turtle's cultural significance and life history in more depth than other animals of the shore. Palauans use the shell of the hawksbill turtle *Eretmochelys imbricata (ngasech)* to make small trays. These turtle shell trays have become, among Palauan women, a medium of exchange and a symbol of recognition for services performed during customs. They are called *toluk*, women's money. Large *toluk* are very valuable.

Sea turtles depend upon the beach to lay and incubate their eggs. A famous Palauan legend describes the turtle's egg-laying cycle. Once upon a time, there were two lovers who met

A horizontal limb of the *"btaches"* tree overhangs the beach on one of the Rock Islands. These trees grow to amazing size in the sandy beach soils next to the water and thrive on the salty environment. A wonderful shade tree.

on the Island of *Ngemelis*. The young woman took off her grass skirt and placed it on a nearby rock. As the night progressed the two lovers made love and began to prepare to return to their respective villages only to find that the skirt had disappeared. She quickly fashioned a substitute skirt but before leaving the two lovers agreed to meet again on *Ngemelis* Island in two weeks time. Upon their return the enchantment of the island embraced them. As they sat on the beach a noise alerted them and upon investigation they saw a hawksbill turtle coming ashore to lay her eggs. Ensnared in the turtles leg was the original grass skirt. In the darkness of their original encounter the young woman had mistaken the back of the turtle for a rock. It was thus that the two lovers discovered that hawksbill turtles return to the same beach every two weeks to lay their eggs.

Hawksbill turtles, *Eretmochelys imbricata (ngasech)* make

Leaves of the mangrove swamp *Nypa* palm are used as roofing material for one of the many "summer houses" that dot Palauan villages.

Coconut leaves are used to make baskets to bring island produce to market.

may lay eighty to one hundred eggs at a time. Newly laid eggs are about the size of a ping pong ball with a soft shell. For seven to twelve weeks, the fertilized eggs incubate in the warm sands. The eggs calcify and harden. The female turtle returns about two weeks later to lay another clutch or set of eggs - as the lovers discovered at *Ngemelis* Island.

The beaches of the Southwest Islands are nesting sites for the green turtle, *Chelonia mydas (melob)*. The green turtle has a smoother and more rounded mouth and shell than the hawksbill. Each year, 50 to 150 turtles nest at *Merir* Island and 10 to 20 turtles nest at Helen's Reef. Less than 5 turtles make their nests at the Islands of *Tobi, Pulo Anna, Sonsorol,* and *Fana* each year. Green turtles nest sporadically year round, with peaks in July and August. Green turtles lay about 100 eggs that incubate for nearly two months. In the Pacific, scientists think green turtles are highly migratory com-

approximately 120-180 nests each year in Palau. The hawksbill turtle has a mouth shaped like a hawk's bill and a rough edged shell. About half of all their nests are within the *Ngerukewid* Island Reserve, a group of Rock Islands in the southern lagoon known as "The Seventy Islands." Palauans find other nests scattered throughout the Rock Island beaches. Turtle nesting occur year round but peak during the summer. A turtle

This large adult Green turtle came ashore, presumably to lay eggs. A timid animal, it quickly swam away when I approached.

Hawksbill hatchling swims in the shallow water off the Southeastern end of *Babelomekang* Island vulnerable to predators in the sky and the sea. Few make it to maturity.

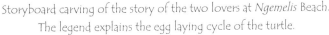
Storyboard carving of the story of the two lovers at *Ngemelis* Beach.
The legend explains the egg laying cycle of the turtle.

pared to the hawksbill, the least migratory species.

Natural weather conditions, physical obstacles and predators determine the fate of turtle eggs and hatchlings. Too much shade, rain or moisture slows down egg development. Fresh water causes eggs to rot. Warm sands produce more female turtles. Cool sands produce more males that incubate longer. Roots surrounding nests hinder the escape of hatchlings. Crabs, birds, large fish, sharks and people eat most of the eggs and hatchlings. As a young girl, my mother-in-law, Ngemelas once watched as a kingfisher *Todirhamphus chloris teraokai (tengadidik)* swooped down to catch a baby hawksbill. Sharks swim near shore and feast on the hatchlings. Knowledgeable hunters calculate when a hawksbill turtle returns to lay eggs. They can distinguish between a turtle's first, intermediate and last clutch. A turtle's first clutch has small, misshapen eggs at the bottom of a nest. These eggs have

little yolk and seldom hatch. Intermediate clutches have few misshapen eggs. The last clutch has small and misshapen eggs on the top rather than the bottom of the nest. The egg clutches are like the first and last pancakes on the morning grill.

The complete life cycle of turtles remains a mystery, although there is some anecdotal information supplied by fishermen. When and where do turtles mate? (My husband, Clarence, saw two green turtles mating in *Melekeok's* ocean waters during February 1997, a day after the new moon.) How long after mating do females lay eggs? Do female turtles return to the same beach year after year? Where do the young turtles live? (As a young boy, Clarence saw turtles the size of his fist in the blue holes of the fringing reefs and in other areas around Palau. He has not seen small turtles in recent years.) I never saw a very small turtle in the wild. Although

The beach at the Northern tip of *Kayangel* Island is, in my opinion, one of the most exquisite places on earth.

Ulong Beach, a favorite stopover between dives.

fishermen still find large turtles in northern *Babeldaob*, turtles are much less common than in the past.

Surveys in the Southwest Islands, Rock Islands, *Babeldaob* and *Kayangel* suggest that turtle populations are decreasing. Scientists report that the endangered green and hawksbill turtle populations need worldwide protection. The turtle's meat and its eggs are a delicacy. Chiefs and high-ranking clan members ate turtles' eggs in the past. Unfortunately, some Palauans still hunt and eat turtle eggs. Palauans raid about seventy percent of the hawksbill turtle nests each year. In Palau it is illegal to kill a turtle on shore or take its eggs. Conservation officers now protect beaches where turtles actively nest. Turtles caught at sea must have a shell size greater than twenty-seven inches for hawksbill turtles and thirty-four inches for green turtles. Palauans cannot hunt sea turtles of any size during the summer (June 1 to August 31) and winter (December 1 to January 31). These laws give sea turtles a chance to lay eggs before being harvested in the fall and spring. The challenge for traditional chiefs is to maintain their cultural heritage without losing the sea turtles forever.

While walking along a beach edge, you may see a rare visitor, the Micronesian Megapode, *Megapodius laperouse (bekai).* The megapode resembles a small brown chicken and makes one of the largest nests in the world. The nests are up to six feet high and twenty-four feet wide! You can miss these well-camouflaged mounds of soil and dead leaves hidden between the trees. The megapode builds its mound by scratching sand and soil with its feet, propelling it backward behind it with rapid strokes of its

legs. It lays its egg on a thick layer of dead leaves which is then covered by more dead leaves and finally with a deep blanket of sand. The heat generated by the decay and composting of the dead vegetation aids in the incubation of the egg. Each mound serves as nest for many megapodes over a period of years. *Kayangel* Atoll has one of the largest populations of megapodes. Megapode mounds are found in southeastern *Babeldaob*, the barrier Islands of *Ngemelis* and *Ulong*, and on several Rock Islands of Koror. Thirty years ago, active megapode nests were found on almost all sandy beaches of the Rock Islands. The megapode egg, like the turtle egg, was a delicacy for high clan chiefs and are about double the size of a chicken egg. Palauan women know how to feel around the nesting mound for the warmest area to find the egg. Ngemelas collected many megapod eggs in her youth. Her mother collected the eggs for her when she was pregnant. Palauans did not kill the megapod because it laid such delicious eggs.

White beach clams, *Atactodea* spp. *(chesechol),* no bigger than your thumbnail, live just below the surface of the sand at the water's edge. Palauan women use their fingers or toes to sift hundreds of these tiny white clams. They boil the clams with coconut milk to make a delicious soup. We made *chesechol* soup after a few hours of collecting in *Ngkeklau* in 1998.

Two types of land crabs, the black *Cardisoma hirtipes (rekung a beluu)* and the brown *Cardisoma carnifex (rekung a daob)* live near the beach. Adult crabs are fist size and live in holes in the forest floor. Crabs are active at night. Small delicate tracks mark their nocturnal forays. Palauans find land crabs year round, but especially during late spring and summer. Land crabs use the beaches as a corridor to the sea, where they release their fertilized eggs. Each egg has a fully developed larvae curled inside and

ready to hatch. *Cardiosoma hirtipes* release their eggs during the full moon. *Cardiosoma carnifex* release their eggs three days after full moon and new moon. Egg bearing females emerge from their holes at dusk and migrate to the sea. The female crabs have many eggs tucked under their abdomen. Once they reach the water's edge, the crabs release the ripened eggs by vigorous flapping of their abdomen. Scientists believe that crabs release their larvae at spring tides to maximize dispersal.

Once caught the crabs are placed in discarded cement bags for the ride back to the house. Then they are put in a chicken wire cage or go directly into the pot.

Land crabs are very lively and can administer a painful bite to the unwary.

Brown land crab.

I have fond memories of catching land crabs in Peleliu. During the evening of full moon, I gathered together with women and children. We each had a sack, a flashlight and a stick. We all jumped into the back of a pick-up truck and drove to the spot where the land crabs were abundant. Once we spotted the crabs, we jumped

from the truck to collect them. We walked along the beach or roads near the shore. We found crabs near tree trunks, under the leaves or along the water's edge. A threatened crab postures itself with both claws extended. Less experienced children use their feet to stop the crab and then grab it from behind to avoid the claws. Experienced children just quickly grab the back of a crab. The crabs can give a painful pinch, so everybody was careful! We placed the captured crabs into small cages of chicken wire. We fed the crabs broken pieces of coconut meat and leaves until it was time for a feast. Stuffed land crabs are delicious. Palauans break each crab exoskeleton (crustaceans have a skeleton outside rather than inside the body) and extract its meat. This is a tedious job. They cook the crabmeat with coconut milk and stuff it back into the crab's carapace or "shell." Palauans eat stuffed crabs *(ukaeb)*

Coconut crabs like this one are found on many Rock Islands. Timid and light sensitive, they are caught at night by leaving an opened coconut near a crack in the limestone wall of a Rock Island and returning later with a flashlight.

Skittish little "ghost" crab darts about the beach just out of reach. When alarmed, they run with amazing speed to the protective shelter of their home, a predug hole in the wet sand.

frequently at feasts in Peleliu, *Angaur* and *Ngaraard*...the lands of beaches.

In 1995, I did some crabbing while living at *Ulimang, Ngaraard.* I had flashbacks of my Peleliu experiences. Each full and new moon, we looked for land crabs along the beaches. Summer time was the best time to collect land crabs because there were so many! During July's full moon, we went out to catch *Cardiosoma hirtipes (rekung a beluu).* *Cardiosoma hirtipes.* These crabs are black in color and spawn during the full moon. We caught 58 crabs in just 20 minutes! During September's full moon we had a crab hunt. Thirty American college students divided into five teams led by a Palauan. We had one rule: nobody could bring back a female crab with eggs. We caught 136 crabs in one

Great Crested Terns lay their eggs in the sand of Helen Reef in the Southwest Islands. The eggs are so prolific it is impossible to walk among them without stepping on some yet the mother always returns to her own egg.

hour's time! We put the crabs into cages and prepared for a tasty dinner the next night. During a spring evening, I walked from *Ulimang* to a hill in *Chelab* to watch the moon rise. At certain spots along the road, dozens of crabs crossed in front of me heading toward the ocean. It

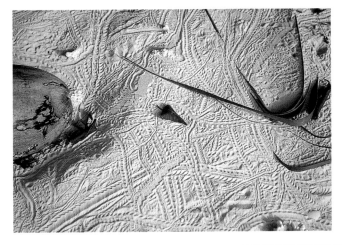

Tracks of the hermit crab provide intricate designs in the soft, dry sand of the Rock Islands.

the collecting of land crabs during the full moon periods in order to conserve this valuable resource.

The coconut crab, *Birgus latro (ketat)* is a giant tarantula like crab that grows to the size of a basketball. The coconut crab takes four to eight years to mature and can live up to fifty years! This crab is the most threatened crab on the island because it is highly sought after and takes so long to mature. Studies show that a mature crab weighs less than a pound and has a carapace width of three to five inches. The weights of a twelve and thirty-year old crabs were about one and four pounds respectively. Coconut crabs can weigh up to nine pounds–about the weight of a small turkey! The coconut crab breeds from

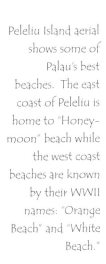

Peleliu Island aerial shows some of Palau's best beaches. The east coast of Peleliu is home to "Honeymoon" beach while the west coast beaches are known by their WWII names: "Orange Beach" and "White Beach."

Photo by Coral Reef Research Foundation

looked like a small traffic jam as the crabs crossed the road one by one. I wondered why certain spots were so busy and what happened when a vehicle passed at this time. I imagined a sign reading "Slow Down–Crab Crossing Ahead." The chiefs of *Chelab* recently banned

May to September, with a peak during July and August. One month before it is ready to release eggs, the crab moves near the shore. The crabs release their eggs into the sea. After about 5-weeks the larvae settle. Juveniles live in a sea shell and become a water dweller. The young crab

will carry a shell until about nine months. When the crabs become more land orientated they discard their adopted sea shells. At night, you can hear these crabs rustling in the leaves. Crab hunters place aluminum cans on sticks to mark their traps baited with coconut meat. You see the markers along the edges of the Rock Islands. Palauans tie captured crabs to posts or put them into cages. They feed them daily with coconuts. Local laws limit the harvest size of coconut crabs, so they have a chance to breed.

What would a beach be without

The soft white beach at *Ngermeas* is frequented by tourists and is a perfect place for water sports.

beach, with all its eggs and all the birds, you cannot help wonder if a few eggs become mixed up during the busy breeding season. Just about any sand bar or beach has shore birds that come to rest and quickly fly away when approached.

Each beach tells a different tale. Peleliu's large expansive beaches have metal wreckage from World War II half-buried in the sands. Large waves crash on the reefs leading up to the sands of White and Orange Beach. Unsettling images flash through my mind as I wander along the quiet shores. The

shore birds visiting now and then? Birds come to the beaches to rest or find food in the sand. There is a sand bar at *Kayangel* where dozens of sandpipers rest. The great crested tern, *Sterna bergii (roall)* nest in large colonies in the spring on exposed sand at Helen's Reef in the Southwest Islands and on *Ngeruangel* Island north of *Kayangel*. A pair of birds has only one egg. As you look at the

ironwood, *Casuarina esquisetifolia (ngas)* whistles softly in the wind. Eeriness fills me when I think of the beaches' bloody past. Lee Marvin beach of *Ngerengchol* Island, Koror, is named after the actor, Mr. Lee Marvin who starred in the movie "Hell in the Pacific," filmed on this beach in the late 1960's. The movie depicts two soldiers, an American and Japanese, stranded on a beach during

200 meter sand spit at the tip of *Ngerebelas* Island in the *Kayangel* atoll.

tour boats speed through. Palauans know the best time. During low tide, we explore the vast expanse of sand. Once we hiked along the more treacherous windward shore. There are small pockets of beach and a forest of ironwood trees with needle-like leaves that carpet the jagged limestone. One late afternoon, a group of us gathered a huge pile of firewood on the sandbar that stretches across to another small island. In the early evening, we lit the firewood during the incoming tide. The water surrounded the blaze as we sang and danced. It was as if we had set fire to the lagoon as water enveloped the flames. As the night progressed, our flames simmered. Midnight's low tide exposed a vast expanse of sand that we walked for hours under the stars.

The beach of *Ulong* Island holds many secrets of past adventures. Scattered pottery shards are remnants of a former village. Ancient pictographs are found on the cliff walls. A memorial commemorates

In this photograph, taken in 1992, the sandy beach reaches out in a graceful arc near *Ulimang*. The beach has since moved to be reformed in another place along the Eastern coast of *Babeldaob*.

World War II. Near shore there are two stone platforms and pottery shards, remnants of one of the original settlement areas of Palauans. The rocky shore has a large population of *Nerite* snails and lots of nooks and crannies to explore.

Most beaches bring back happy memories of picnics and camping trips with friends and family. *Ngemelis* is home to my favorite beaches. (Camping at *Ngemelis* Island is possible if you receive a permit from Koror State.) There are large beaches and reefs on *Ngemelis* as well as old settlements within the forests. During a morning incoming tide schools of silverfish, *Gerres oyena (chesall)* come in and a few small black tip sharks. You can drift along the inner channel's current between the islands. Along the way, there are a colorful array of coral and fish and an occasional shark. Snorkel after or before

Captain Wilson, the famous English captain whose ship, the Antelope, crashed onto the nearby reefs. One morning I swam amongst the schools of silversides at sunrise. During different visits to *Ulong* beach I saw hundreds of lavender jellyfish and blue stinging jellyfish *(siphonophores)* swept along the shore. The flowers of *Barringtonia asiatica (btuul)* cover the sand with an explosion of pink filaments. Its large, four-angled green fruit turns brown and drops to the ground looking like a popover.

I spent lunch hours on this beach while doing surveys of grouper populations in the nearby *Ulong* Channel.

Our family camped on *Ulong* Island 3 or 4 times. I will never forget one New Year's weekend with the Pathfinders Club. Some students made rockets for their honor project. On New Year's Eve, we went to the beach to watch as they set off their rockets. One student made a rocket 4 times larger than the rest. All the smaller rockets went straight up in the air and

A bonfire is a great ending to a full day in the sun.

sparkled the night sky. They saved the largest rocket for last. I stood back, fearful of what would happen. We watched in surprise as the rocket skidded along the sand, skimmed over the water and went straight up into the air. What a light show we had that New Year's Eve.

Once we walked along *Ngaraard's* long stretch of eastern beach from *Choll* to *Ulimang*. It was a great afternoon adventure. We found red-ribbed shells of the giant clam, *Hippopus hippopus (duadeb)*. We waded among brown seagrass clumps and filamentous algae along the beach. We examined pieces of crustaceans and fish and shells of all kinds. Shade trees like *Calophyllum inophyllum (btaches)*, the lantern tree, *Hernandia sonora (doko)* and the coconut tree, *Cocos nucifera (lius)* offered cool refuge from the hot sands. After a rain, small streams of cold water ran intermittently from the forest to the beach. At the streams we sat with our feet dangling in the cool water and rested under shade trees. At various points along the beach large volcanic outcrops jutted out with water trickling down their steep walls from the grassland above. As we walked, the coastline transformed from lowland coconut plantations to steep vertical walls of volcanic rocks. Clusters of Nerite snails hid in small crevices of the volcanic rocks. As the tide came in we moved quickly around the large rocks before the tidal

waters covered the beaches. That evening we watched the full moon, ever so large and splendid, rise over *Ngaraard's* eastern horizon.

Kayangel's beaches offer a different kind of solitude and peace. Red coral, *Tubipora muscia*, blue coral, *Heliopora coerula*, and top shells, *Trochus niloticus (semum)* decorate the windward beaches. Ghost crabs *(chesechuul)* nervously run to and from their holes. Seagrasses thrive in the lagoon and wash ashore. In the past, glass fishing balls washed ashore from distant ships. Now, plastics, Styrofoam, zories and aluminum wash ashore. The low tide exposes a sand bar at *Ngerebelas* Island,

Eoulomekang beach is isolated, pristine and totally natural.

beach, men cast for jacks and snappers. Our children build their own campsite on this apex of windblown sand. They chatter through the night while their parents sleep. We watch our children grow on the beaches. Together we learn to swim, fish, build a fire, make friends and share in the joy of endless sand.

People love a beach, a timeless place to walk and think. Rhythmic waves lap against the shore and are transformed into a gentle hiss of bubbles. At any given moment, waves erase the sand and imprints disappear. The beach becomes a fresh canvas for nature's art. We must take care not to change the delicate balance between shore life and its sandy home. Let the beaches be shaped only by nature's course.

REFERENCES

Engbring, J. 1988. *Field Guide to the Birds of Palau.*

Maragos, J.E. 1994. *Marine and Coastal Areas Survey of the Main Palau Islands. Part 2.* CORIAL Honolulu, Hawaii. The Nature Conservancy Pacific Region.

Nichols, P.V. 1991. *Republic of Palau Marine Resources Profiles. FFA Report No. 91/59* South Pacific Forum Fisheries Agency. Solomon Islands.

Reese, E. S. 1971. Background information and recommendation for a programme of management and conservation of the coconut crab, *Birgus latro*, in the Trust Territory of the Pacific Islands.

Whistler, A. 1992. *Flowers of the Pacific Island Seashore.*

"Footprints in the sand."

Kayangel. It is a unique place to be. The windward side of this narrow sand bar has a steep bank with deep water and wave action. Within a few seconds, you can run across to the calm, warm lagoon waters. Once my friend Linda Subris fished with a line while I swam in the waves on the windward side. Suddenly, she got a bite. She struggled and brought in baby blacktip shark! Along the

Atolls

An atoll is a ring of coral that embraces a shallow lagoon. The naturalist, Charles Darwin explained that an atoll was once a volcanic island with a fringing reef. Over millions of years, the island slowly sank. The growth of the fringing reef kept pace with the sinking island. Eventually the fringing reef formed a ring of coral and a shallow lagoon replaced the sunken island. The sea level continued to drop, so part of the coral ring became exposed. We can imagine an atoll as the last effort of a drowning volcano to lift its head above water.

Palau has atolls. The two northern atolls are *Ngeruangel* and *Kayangel* and the southwest atoll is Helen Reef. *Ngeruangel* Atoll is uninhabited and about 5.5-miles northwest of *Kayangel*. *Ngeruangel* Atoll is a submerged reef, except for one small islet. Shore birds and green turtles nest and breed on the islet. The fishing is great in its surrounding waters. *Kayangel* Atoll is 25 miles north of *Babeldaob* and populated with 150 residents. *Kayangel* Atoll is about 4.5 miles long and 2 miles wide and has four small vegetated islands on its south eastern side. The islands decrease in size from north to south and are named as follows:

Kayangel, Ngeriungs, Ngerebelas and *Orak* Islands.

The Southwest Islands are made up of six widely dispersed islands: *Fanna, Sonsorol, Pulo Anna, Merir, Tobi* and Helen Reef. These Islands are a few hundred miles southwest of Palau's mainland archipelago and have about 80 residents. Five islands formed on the reefs. The fringing reef flats and slopes face the open sea. Helen Reef is an atoll that is part of *Tobi* Island. Helen Reef has the largest reef system in the southwest and the greatest diversity of marine life. Helen is a wild place where seabirds blacken the skies during nesting time and tuna bite your line within a minute's time. Nesting birds, turtles, giant clams, fish and other marine life are plentiful. A true adventure awaits us at the Southwest Islands.

On a clear day, you can see *Kayangel* from a high vantage point in *Ngaraard* and *Ngarchelong*. We must plan in advance for a trip to *Kayangel*. We pack camping equipment and enough food for an overnight stay. A day trip to *Kayangel* is possible but to really enjoy *Kayangel* you should spend the night. In the 1970's the only transportation to *Kayangel* was on the traditional

Kayangel Atoll.

Constantly pounded by a never-ending procession of ocean waves, the small islands are protected by the barrier reef. There are places on the east side of *Kayangel* where the reef is less than 200 yards (200 meters) wide.

Our drivers on the smaller boats are less anxious about the open sea with the large boats nearby. On one trip we even had a jet ski trailing along!

During the journey we get an overview of Palau's size and shape. We realize

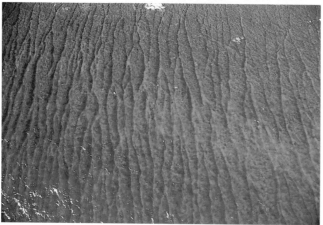

The underwater reef surface is a series of ridges and channels etched by the coming and going of the tides.

Trips to *Kayangel* aboard an old wooden boat, called bilas by Palauans, could take a full day. The slow trip provided lots of time to relax, trade stories and troll for fish.

bilas. (A *"bilas"* is a boat made of wood with an inboard diesel engine.) It was a one-day journey. Today, large twin engine boats can get to *Kayangel* within two hours. While traveling over rough seas, the view of *Kayangel* in the distance calms anxious passengers. During heavy rains and rough seas, only experienced boaters travel between *Babeldaob* and *Kayangel*.

I have shared several memorable adventures with friends on trips to *Kayangel*. We meet at the dock in the early morning. Once the boats and people are ready, the boats leave the dock one by one. Our entourage of large and small boats heads up the coast. Large boats carry women and small children. Small boats with older children and men zoom ahead or behind the large boats.

that Koror (an area of 9.3 square kilometers) is really a series of many islands connected by bridges and causeways. *Babeldaob* is the largest island in Palau (an area of 332 square kilometers—second only to Guam in Micronesia). The main boat route travels along the western and northern lagoon.

Abandoned coconut plantations checker the hillsides along *Babeldaob's* west coast. Mangroves and intermittent stone jetties built through the mangroves and over the fringing reefs trim the shore. Large volcanic rocks thrust upward towards the sky in *Ngeremlengui*. The abrupt landscape transforms into gentle hills in *Ngardmau*. In *Ngardmau* a small shelter perched atop *Ngarchelus* mountain marks the highest point in Palau, 721 feet above sea level.

While traveling along *Babeldaob's* coast, the legend of Palau's violent creation comes to my mind. Once there was a woman named *Latmikaik,* whose mother was a large clam *(kim). Latmikaik* gave birth to four children on *Angaur* Island. Her first son was named *Uab. Uab* was an unusual child who grew very fast and consumed great quantities of food. He quickly became a giant, so huge that the villagers could not satisfy his insatiable appetite. Finding they could no longer feed him the villagers became frightened and decided they must kill him. He was tied up

This long sand spit on *Ngerebelas* Island disappears into the emerald green waters of the lagoon.

113

Swimming in water so clear and warm is a soothing and magical experience.

amidst huge piles of wood which were then set on fire. *Uab's* huge body exploded scattering his body parts all over the sea, and as legend has it, thus created the Palau Islands. *Uab's* chest became the west coast, his knees formed *Airai* and his groin became *Aimeliik*. *Uab's* stomach was to become *Ngiwal* and *Uab's* head formed the northern tip of *Babeldaob*. Palauans attribute the character of villages to parts of the giant *Uab.* For example, in *Ngiwal* the people eat seven times a day.

While in route, you may see the large rock borders of the western barrier reef, exposed during low tide. The barrier reef acts as a buffer against the open ocean waves breaking over the reef. *Ngardmau's* lagoon has rough water because this is a narrow section of lagoon where a channel cuts through the barrier reef. Otherwise, the calm western lagoon acts as a haven for our entourage of boats. When our boats exit the northern lagoon we enter an

immense area of shallow open water surrounded by four large reefs. At *Kossol* Reef we drive through a passage that leads to the open sea. Now, waves may crash against the boat and cause it to roll. No barrier reefs exist to break the impact of the waves' force. The large unpredictable waves are exciting and frightening all at once. Spinner dolphins pass as flying fish cruise above the water's surface. Sea birds begin to follow behind the boat. We sight *Kayangel* and our eyes fixate on its image. I gaze

The clear deep blue color of the *Kayangel* lagoon is unforgettable.

Kayangel's west coast is one long continuous beach that dips gently into the lagoon.

The east and west coasts of *Kayangel* are distinctly different. The west coast shores are soft and sandy and extend into the lagoon. The east coast is rocky with the sand pushed up to the shoreline as a result of the more violent wave action.

into the endless horizon around me but always fix my eyes back on the atoll.

The entrance into *Kayangel's* lagoon is breathtaking and unforgettable. The deep navy blue ocean becomes an aqua green blue lagoon embraced by white sands. The stunning beauty teases every amateur photographer. The atoll is a magical oasis floating on an immense sea. The peaceful lagoon is a welcome sight to weary adventurers. We head for

Kayangel's east coast looks more like a moonscape than a tropical island.

Ngerebelas, our favorite island. Upon arrival, we form a human chain across the beach. We unload our camping equipment and supplies and then begin to explore. The bright sun on the white sand blinds us. The water's waves create elongated sand waves on the beach.

There is a sense of freshness as your footprints leave the first afternoon trail. The fine sands massage your feet as

Ngeruangel Atoll is a favorite place to harvest trochus *shells.* Trochus *season only comes once evey couple of years. Shells over 3-inches may be taken and sold to buyers from foreign lands who use them to make buttons.*

circling the atoll. During low tide, the exposed beaches form a path that connects the four islands in the atoll.

Kayangel's beaches are among the best in Palau. The North beach of *Ngerbelas* Island has my favorite sand spit (a narrow sand beach extending outward from the island). Within seconds I can run from the wave swept windward shore to the tranquil lagoon side, a place that offers a change of nature and emotions. Upon my approach the sea birds stop their chatter and fly off their end of the sand spit. Over the next days their flights become less sudden and frequent. It is the only beach where ghost crabs chase me. Ocean waves strike the exposed sandstone coastline and beach of *Orak* Island. Turtles were once common nesters along *Orak's* beaches. The main island of *Kayangel* is the largest island with long stretches of beach lined with coconut trees. As I wander through the atoll forest I notice that some coconut trees barely stand. The wind and storms caused the sand to erode away from the roots. In the island's interior the agroforests include papayas and about seven types of bananas. The yellow hibiscus, *Hibiscus tiliaceous (chermall)* is a special plant because it is part of the legend of *Kayangel's* birth.

you walk. Till now, sandpipers, ghost crabs and wandering mollusks left the only prints in the sand. Driftwood, finely sculptured by wind and wave, is show-cased against a blue sky. The sculpted wood captures light from hidden angles through-out the day. Frigate birds soar high in the air,

Ngeruangel Atoll.

Ngeruangel Atoll is a rocky, barren sand hill inhabited by birds.

While exploring I noticed that the windward and leeward coasts of the islands are quite different. The windward side has large boulders and coral fragments. The shoreline is shaped by the force of large ocean blown waves. The beaches are full of the sea's remnants. Scattered pieces of the red organ pipe coral *Tubipora muscia* are everywhere. The blue coral, *Heliopora coerulea* is a "living fossil" whose ancestors can be traced back to the Mesozoic era. The red streaked white shells of the giant clam *Hippopus hippopus (duadeb)* lie here and there in the sands. The top shell *Trochus nilocticus (semum)* is also white streaked in red. Thick purple spines of the pencil urchin *Heterocentrotus mammillatus* are a lucky find. In the past, glass fishing balls washed ashore from foreign fishing nets. Colored glass fragments mix with shells and seaweeds. Beachcombers, young and old, show off and exchange their newly found treasures. Creative minds begin to imagine new jewelry and ornaments.

The leeward beaches accumulate deep layers of sand along the lagoon edge. A swim in the warm lagoon waters is soothing. Once within the lagoon I peer through the liquid blue while swimming over white sands. Fish and sea cucumbers hide between blades of seagrass. A few very large corals lie scattered in the lagoon. It is pleasant to swim around and among the huge coral heads. Brilliant red, yellow, orange and candy striped Christmas worms embed themselves in the giant massive coral heads of

Backbone segment of a large whale on *Ngeruangel.*

Porites lutea. (The worms appear as miniature Christmas trees made of colored pipe cleaners twisted into shape in an arts and crafts class.) I venture farther toward the reef front near *Ulach* Channel. The reef front is a garden of robust and stunted corals that can withstand the sea's incessant pounding. There are no delicate hard corals, soft corals or sponges at the reef front. The strong currents by the outer lagoon and reef front can carry you out to sea. Seek the advice of the

village chiefs first before you venture too far. I was out with college students who were experienced swimmers. Before we knew it, they were all being carried out to sea by the strong current. Luckily we were all safe. We learned to respect the currents of the lagoon that day.

Casting and line fishing is exciting along the shore. Once my friend caught a baby blacktip shark on our line just near the sand spit! We admired it and returned it to the sea. (I swam a bit closer to shore after that.) Gung ho fisherfolk troll, cast and spear fish. They are out for the big catch. They head to the northern submerged atoll of *Ngaruangel* or outside *Kayangel's* reefs. (You must first get permission from the *Kayangel* chiefs to fish in their waters. These areas are now sanctuaries.) The fishermen brought back big jacks, wahoo and barracuda for barbecue. We take home coolers full of fish to freeze or share with friends. Some

boats head over to *Kayangel* Island for a few hours to visit with the chief and pick up some ice at their ice making plant. The fishermen spend hours, day and night, telling fishing tales. They discuss their fishing preparations weeks before. Each year they want to catch the fish that eluded them the year before. Adult lifeguards take turns onshore. An emergency boat stays moored near shore. Fishermen go out day and night until every cooler is full. During the day fishermen troll and cast. At night they handline, spearfish or hunt for lobsters. *Kayangel* is a fisherman's paradise.

Kayangel's beaches are magical in the moonlight. One evening we gazed in wonder at a partial eclipse of the moon! Bright stars sparkle and gentle breezes whisper through the trees. The moon sends its beam across the calm lagoon waters and over the white sands. As day turns to night, families continue to eat fresh fish and listen to more tales. A few

Ngeruangel Atoll at low tide.

A small, close community, the children of *Kayangel* spend sunny days together on the beach after school and on weekends. Once out of elementary school, they will live in Koror with relatives and attend high school returning to *Kayangel* on weekends and holidays.

visitors from the main village of *Kayangel* Island may stop by and visit. Our older children find their special spot. Together, they make a thatched roof propped up with tree branches. They use coconut leaves for flooring. They feed their fires, while telling stories late into the night. Simple tasks now defy the ticking clocks back home. It is hard to sleep in *Kayangel* on a moonlit night. We want the night to last forever. Older parents seem content to chat a few hours more. The ocean waves calm the night. Parents with young children are asleep. Families set up their tents on the lagoon side of the island, where the winds are calmer. Warm blankets, rhythmic lapping of waves against the shore and gentle breezes eventually put most to sleep. There are a few that never sleep. At dawn the cool air, a pink sky and smells of a burning fire and hot coffee awaken us. Some take a quick morning dip or a quiet walk along the shore to contemplate. It is not just the beaches, lagoon or the fishing. The whole island captures you. You are the only people for miles around.

There is always the longing to stay just one more day. The enthusiastic, never tiring few take one last fishing trip, swim or walk. Then everybody gets together to pack and clean. Mothers search for the children's zoris, shirts and towels that are nowhere to be found. We form a human chain. We load up gear for the trip home. An entourage of boats heads out of *Ulach* Passage one by one. Only a bamboo stick marks the entrance. As we leave the

passage, the open sea greets us. Once over *Kossol* Reef, the boaters relax as they speed through the northern lagoon and along the west cost of *Babeldaob* once more. The trip home seems faster. Most passengers nap a bit. Once back at the dock we unload our gear. Before we all go our separate ways we divide the fish between families. Memories of the trip linger as we clean and pack away our things for the next adventure. During one Thanksgiving feast we got together to eat and watch a "*Kayangel* video" made by our friend, Margo. Bits and pieces of the adventure came alive once more.

So, what is an atoll? A tropical microcosm shared by few. A ring of coral embracing emerald blue water. An oasis that's hard to get to and hard to leave. A mystical place with striking hues and textures. A land of beaches with few foot prints and many hidden treasures. A magical spot with starlit nights and fishing adventures. A paradise that beckons us to days of peaceful solitude.

REFERENCES

Maragos J. et al. 1994. *Marine and Coastal Areas Survey of the Main Palau Islands.* Part 2. Rapid Ecological Assessment Synthesis Report. CORIAL Honolulu Hawaii and The Nature Conservancy Pacific Region.

Art of Palau

The creation of a simple handmade tool to the construction of the magnificent bai is Palauan art. A simple tool, like an adze, is a blend of skill and creativity to admire and use. An artisan makes his adze by selecting the best quality wood for its handle and shell for its blade. The artisan skillfully ties together the newly sculptured handle and blade. In turn he uses his adze to create an entire canoe or a men's *bai.* Artists added beauty to each creation with inlaid shells, low relief carvings and paintings. Palauans used many handcrafted tools to carve wood, make pottery, weave baskets and hunt wildlife and fish. Several types of objects represented symbolic links to the spirits, deities and ancestors who controlled all aspects of daily life.

Artists connect with their natural and spiritual environment. The natural environment provides wood, coconut leaves, *Pandanus* leaves, *Hibiscus* fibers, bark of breadfruit tree, shells, stone, coral, clay and bones. The human body is a medium for the art of tattooing. Palauan society incorporated imported materials with their own natural materials. European ships brought metal objects including firearms,

swords, utensils and pots. The strength and power of metal objects amazed Palauans. They learned to heat and shape metal. They replaced shell adzes with metal adzes, spears of shell with metal spears and shell knives with metal knives. The Spanish ships brought beautiful large ceramic pottery that was less fragile than Palauan pottery. Art is a dynamic process that combines both old and new skills and techniques. Palauans blend new materials and techniques with their own traditional artistry.

The spiritual environment is ever present for artists. Building a *bai* or canoe is a community effort led by a master builder. It is the master builder's responsibility to ensure that both the natural and spiritual conditions are right. The master builder observes many rituals during the process of construction. The master builder begins construction during a specific phase of the moon and recites chants that recognize certain spirits. The master builder sets a natural and spiritual rhythm in motion and sustains it until the project is complete.

The pinnacle of artistic expression is the construction of the *bai,* the meeting house of the traditional

A simple coconut shell when painted makes
an attractive hanging basket for tropical plants.

128

leaders. The *bai* incorporates many forms of art including woodwork, architecture, interior and exterior design, painting, stonework and landscape. Each phase of construction is an arduous task of transporting natural materials, sculpting these materials with handmade tools and fitting it all together. Paintings on the *bai* illustrate the history of the culture. Elaborate stone platforms elevate the *bai*. A network of stone pathways leads to the *bai*. Palauans meticulously placed each stone. Village communities continue to maintain these stone pathways. Palauans portray their view of the world and their place in society through the *bai*. The *Dilukai*, a wooden sculpture or low relief carving of a woman on the

Painted carvings on Palauan *bai* in *Aimeliik* were the original Palauan art form. Traditions, legends and community values were often depicted on the gables of the *bai*.

front gable of the *bai* became a key symbol of Palauan art worldwide.

The *bai* inspired the development of a new art form, the storyboard. Storyboards are portable adaptations of the low relief carvings on the *bai*. During the 1930's, Dr. Hisataku Hijikata, a Japanese anthropologist and artist, encouraged Palauan woodcarvers to produce traditional stories on small boards (*bai* pictographs) for sale and export to Japan. These carved boards are called "storyboards." Artisans developed complex high relief carvings compared to the original low relief carvings. Since the 1930's many master carvers have produced storyboards with unique styles and compositions. In 1980 my husband, Clarence Kitalong, began carving under the tutelage of his Uncle Sbal, a master carver from *Ngetkib, Airai*.

The process of storyboard carving has many steps. The first step is to find an appropriate piece of wood. Friends get a chain saw and truck and drive to a spot where there is

Contemporry form of "*bai* art" adorns the front of The Carolines Resort office.

With the help of these chisels, this piece of raw wood will soon be transformed into a storyboard by the skilled hands of an artist.

tools and maintains them on a regular basis. Carvers order their tools from steel companies in Germany and Switzerland.

Once the board and tools are ready, the artist creates his composition of the story. It may take several days before an artist visualizes his composition. Placement and emphasis of the *bai,* a canoe and the main characters of the legend vary with each theme. Clarence practices drawing figures on a pad before he begins his final composition. An artist's creativity brings a story to life. Once the artist sketches his composition on the wood, he is ready to carve. He shapes the wood with a flattened chisel, then carves in low relief an outline of the basic theme with a narrow V-shaped chisel. He carefully carves the finer details (like the leaves of trees, faces of people and *bai* decor) with a small V-shaped chisel. Once he completes the carving, he sands the whole board with fine sandpaper until it is smooth. He may paint the board with inks of red, white, yellow and

Careful taps with a wooden mallet begin to bring the story to life.

The story is first drawn on the wood with a pencil before carving begins.

either a fallen tree or a good sized tree to cut. The wood is cut into pieces large and small. Large trees are taken to the sawmill. They may cut pieces into smaller planks with a table saw. The carvers sand the rough wood surface by hand or with an electric sander until it is smooth. The hardwood called *Intsia bijuga (dort)* is the most durable wood and can be found on the Rock Islands. Mahogany, *Swietenia mahogani (mahogani),* is a lighter wood that is more manageable to carve. Carvers sharpen their hand tools with a stone block. An artist is meticulous about his

brown. He rubs brown shoe polish into the board to protect the wood and shines it for added luster.

Certain legends are popular and requested often. The Magic Breadfruit tree that produced fish, the Two Lovers of

Here, master carver John Q. Demei etches his design into the wood. He uses an old washing machine wringer as his hammer. When I asked him why, he simply said, "its quieter."

Ngemelis Island who discovered the turtle's egg laying cycle and the story of Natural Child Birth are most popular. An artist may create a contemporary theme from recent events. Some of Clarence's best work was carved in a day. Yet, that one-day of creativity required many days of preparation and practice, as with any recital or performance. Understanding the phases and process of creating gives you a deeper appreciation of this art form. Today storyboards are a major art industry in Palau.

Canoe building is an elaborate artistic process. The master builder has the laborious task of sculpting his canoe from a single tree trunk. He must design a seaworthy craft that is both efficient in function and beautiful in form. He supervises the ornamentation of the canoe as well. Master carvers built and utilized a variety of canoes in Palau. Palauan society highly valued the war canoe, renown for its form, structure and utilitarian design. The design of a canoe was important during war and ceremonial displays. A well-built canoe must maneuver easily in the water and compliment the skills of its paddlers during engagements in time of war.

The finished storyboard tells the Palauan legend of the breadfruit tree. Coated with shoe polish and buffed with a shoe brush the board will be sold in one of Koror's many gift shops.

Palauans still practice the art of spear making. Young boys spear birds, fishermen and hunters spear fish and wildlife for food and warriors once speared each other in battle. Two types of war spears (called *besos* and *cholechodech*) were long, elaborately carved and had a sharpened tip. A young boy first learns to make a dart used with a blowgun. The boys make blowguns using the hollow stem of the plant *Schizostachyum lima (lild)*. The blowgun holds a small dart called the *ulekput*. This dart has a cotton wad at the rear end to secure it inside the blowgun. My children made these in

their youth. Older boys make different types of fishing spears. The body of the spear is made from a thin bamboo called *"lild."* The tip of the spear is made with metal wire. The boys heat the stem of the bamboo to straighten it and then tie on the metal prongs.

Today fishing spears are used on a daily basis and are produced in a variety of configurations. The single pronged spear *(klibiskang)* is used on the reef for rabbitfish and humphead parrotfish. A multipronged spear *(taod)* is effective with yellowtail mullet *(uluu)* and grouper while a smaller spear called *"olaod"* is used for sardines. Making a speargun *(boes ra ngikel)* requires both wood work and metal work. The body of the gun is made from a light wood that will float if it is released underwater. A discarded table fork or spoon is often fashioned into a trigger mechanism.

Palauan fishermen have both throw spears and spearguns for different fishing activities.

The people of *Tobi* are renown for their ability to make fish hooks. They make them *(chirocher)* with bone, shell, metal or wood. The fishermen of these islands still produce handmade hooks. There are thirteen basic hook patterns of which twelve predate the introduction of metal.

A true work of art. Note the mother of pearl inlays that adorn the upper edge.

Other woodwork of Palau included elaborate containers and bowls. The famous British captain, Captain Wilson received as a gift an elaborate wooden container with shell inlay. This container, now in a British Museum, is bird shaped and decorated with small inlaid bird figures. Great prestige was attached to covered inlaid bowls, used for offerings of coconut candy to powerful chiefs. "Money jars" were especially elaborate and held Palauan bead money. The coloring, lacquering and decorating of bowls was exquisite. Palauans painted their pots with red clay and the reddish oil extracted from the fruit of the tree, *Paranari glaberrimum (cheritem)*. The longer you boiled the fruit, the more red the oil became.

Fish, meat, taro and other food and drinks were served in specially crafted bowls. Most wooden pots or plates had flat bottoms. Palauans used special rim bottomed plates to serve taro *(buuk)* and fish *(ongall)*. The artist *Renguul* of Peleliu carved a serving bowl for fish. This polished bowl made from ironwood, *Intsia bijuga (dort)* was on display at the National Museum of Natural History, Washington D.C. A large bowl called *"ilengel"*

was used for drinking a sweet syrup mixture and a specially shaped bowl known as *"orsachel"* served as a container for pounding medicine and betelnut.

Today wooden containers and sculptures like the famous *Dilukai* are uncommon. Woodcarvers make "monkey men" and miniature *bai* for tourists. Private art collectors request artists to produce specific types of sculptured woodwork. In the past, large canoe house *(diangel)* support posts were carved in the shape of human figures. The people from *Tobi* island made coffins

Ornately carved dishes of *Airai* chief *"Ngiraked."* Only *"Ngiraked"* could eat from these dishes.

from mangrove wood. After a funeral, they brought the coffin to the beach, placed it in a canoe and set it adrift.

Shells were used to decorate canoes, money jars *(oledabel)* and storyboards. Intricate inlaid designs made use of the mother-of-pearl shell *Pteria martensii (chesiuch)* to beautify wood carvings. Mother-of-pearl was used to make tools for removing the thorny edges of *Pandanas* leaves and a leaf splitter that was used to split the leaves into long strips for basket weaving. Pestles *(chai)* for pounding taro were made from the thick base

Contemporary Palauan artist Sam Adelbai is one of Palau's best mural painters. He has done many large murals, which decorate hotels and commercial buildings in Palau.

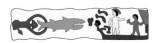

Margo Vitarelli's original batik on cloth characterizes Palauan women collecting clams in the mangrove swamp. The women use their feet to find the clams in the deep mud and bring them to the surface with their toes.

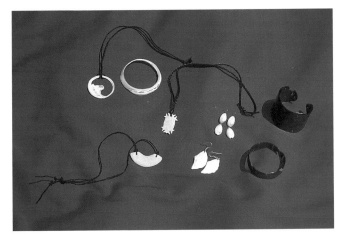

Earrings, bracelets and pendants crafted from seashells and turtle shell by local Palauan artists are sold to tourists.

of the giant clamshell, *Tridacna gigas (otkang)*. Weaving tools, knives, building and carving tools all came from the clam shell. Bracelets were made from the trochus shell *Trochus niloticus (semum)* and earrings were made from the boring clams *Tridacna crocea (oruer)* and *Tridacna derasa (kism)*. Grieving women wore mourning money *(ngatbult)*, a thin rounded piece of mother-of-pearl shell, around their necks. Today local artists continue to produce beautiful shell jewelry.

The shell of the hawksbill turtle, *Eretmochelys imbricata (ngasech)* is the most valued shell in Palau. The entire shell is a series of joined plates, that when boiled, separate easily. The softened plates when sandwiched between

"Women's money" called "toluk" is made from the shell of the Hawksbill turtle. Women receive "toluk" as payment for food preparation services during customs.

opposite halves of a convex wooden mold, form a shallow tray with a raised lip. The finished product is called a *"toluk."* Pre-European *toluk* was highly polished and had small motifs cut into the edges. The *toluk*, originally a serving dish, became women's money. A woman receives a *toluk* from her husband's clan. The *toluk* is payment for her food preparation services during a custom. *Toluk* are a mark of high status. Women collect, carefully wrap and keep their *toluk* in a hidden place. High quality *toluk* are large in size, thick, have a good natural pattern and lack deformities. Shining a dull

128

Woven *Pandanus* baskets made by Senior Citizens. These baskets are called *"tet"* and will be used by Palauans to hold the necessary components for betelnut chewing. Many will be sold to tourists as gifts and souvenirs.

toluk with very fine sandpaper gives it luster. Today large turtles are rare and high quality *toluk* are precious. Smaller parts of the turtle shell were fashioned into dessert dishes, large spoons *(terir)*, rings, earrings, brace-lets and sewing needles. Wearing a series of bracelets *(klilt)* was a sign of wealth for women. Today Palau has a harvest season and size limit for the endangered hawksbill turtles.

Basket weaving is popular among Palauan women. My-mother-in-law, Ngemelas, and her relatives weave baskets. My few attempts have taught me to appreciate the patience and skill it takes to weave even the simplest

Hand woven Christmas tree ornaments made from *Pandanus* leaves.

basket. There are many steps to weaving a basket. The first step is to gather young leaves and dry them. Men may help gather *Pandanus* or coconut leaves for weaving and other leaves for making dyes. When weaving coconut baskets the midrib of the coconut frond is striped away and the leaves cut to size. Each leaflet is woven, in and out, one over the other. Once you get to the corners you pull the leaves together and tie them on the bottom. It can be confusing. Ornaments and baskets with interwoven dyed strips are beautiful creations.

Kayangel woman strips off the thorny outer edges of the *pandanus* leaf. The tool she is using is made from an old WWII canteen. Others make their stirpping tool from seashells.

Palauan baskets include a thin hard vine basket *(saru)*, a large food basket made of the climbing fern, *Lygodium circinatum (ngidech)*, a basket to hold cooked starch *(orekill)*, a fishing basket made of coconut leaves *(chelais)*, a large fishing basket *(cheleuocho)* and a basket with large openings *(bloket)*. A small basket *(oruikl)* is used by men to hold their personal items. Women store their personal effects in a basket called *omsangel*. The most common basket is the *"tet"*, a small woven basket used for holding betel nut, *kebui* leaves, lime *(choas)* and personal items. Palauans use a flat woven container *(chedib)* to hold *kebui* leaves. Many types of woven baskets and purses are available at the Senior Citizen Center, the *Belau* National Museum and other local stores.

There were about two dozen types of grass skirts *(cheriut)* in Palau. Women made skirts with sedge, *Eleocharis* species *(kerdikes)*, the ti plant, *Cordyline* species

(sis), coconut fronds *(lius)*, banana leaves of *Musa textilis (tuu)*, the inner bark of the *Hibiscus* tree, *Hibiscus tiliaceus (chermall)* and other plants. A skirt had a front and back panel tied together at the waist. The panels of the skirt were held together by a *Hibiscus* fiber twine. Skirts were dyed various colors to signify a woman's rank and clan. Yellow came from the ginger plant *Curcuma domestica* and black from the mud of the taro patch. Plain colored skirts, those that are not dyed, were left in the sun to dry without further treatment. Pouches *(otungel)* made of *Pandanus* were sewn in the skirts acting as pockets to hold valuables. A belt with a triangular section of woven *Pandanus* was worn beneath the skirt for purposes of modesty. A dagger made from the stingrays barb was often hidden in the skirt.

Decorative belts were made from sea shells, turtle shell, coconut shell, woven *Pandanus* leaves and sometimes the

skin of the dugong, *Dugong dugong (mesekiu)*. The influence of Yapese culture can be seen in the traditional dress of Southwest Island women during pregnancy. Braided belts made of human hair were worn by young girls until their first pregnancy. A woven belt of *Pandanus* indicated that a woman was pregnant. After delivery, women wore a skirt of woven *Pandanus* with a distinctive rectangular pattern. The *Belau* National Museum, the Etpison Museum and the Bernice Pauahi Bishop Museum have skirts of coconut fiber on display. During celebrations in Palau, women rarely wear the traditional grass skirts. You are more likely to see modern "grass skirts" made with plastics and colorful yarns.

Skirts are made of synthetic fibers and are brightly colored to identify clan or rank. Note the Palauan money worn around the necks of the young girls in the foreground.

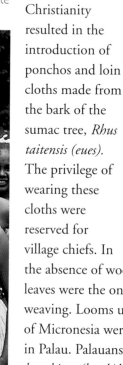

The spread of Christianity resulted in the introduction of ponchos and loin cloths made from the bark of the sumac tree, *Rhus taitensis (eues)*. The privilege of wearing these cloths were reserved for village chiefs. In the absence of wool and yarns, plant leaves were the only material used for weaving. Looms used in other parts of Micronesia were not to be found in Palau. Palauans used *Pandanus kanehirae (buuk)* leaves to make a variety of mats. Burial mats *(badek)*, personal sitting mats *(bruk)*, bedding for guests *(balbai)*, infant mats *(brul a ngalek)*, and mats hung in doorways *(uletech)* are but a few. With the advent of synthetic fibers and mass production, mats imported from abroad have taken the place of the once essential pandanus mat.

Rope was made from the inner fibers of the coconut. The green husk was split into sections and soaked in seawater for about two months. After soaking in the sea, the fibers were sun dried, combed and twisted into

Clay cooking pots (olekang) were common. Palauans used several large cooking pots (kauang, olisall, olongosall, and ongederoall). Coconut syrup was boiled in a pot called oltall. Small pots called ongelidel were used to boil water. Water bottles had a small slender neck and a large belly resembling the megapode bird. Both the bird and the bottle are called bekai. Earthen pots had rounded bottoms, no handles or legs and differed only in size and the ratio between the depth and size of the lip. Water bottles, which could be quite large, had lips that curved inward and were often decorated with distinctive patterns. Clay lanterns (olbidel) were produced in a shape that suggested a strong European influence.

The creation of pottery has many phases. First a potter needs clay in order to make a pot. Ibobang and Oikull are areas known for good quality clay. The best clay is pale brown in color and found beneath the red clay

These dancers wear grass skirts made of young coconut leaves for their dance in front of the bai.

string. Two strands of string were woven together to become a single strand of rope (blades) that was then rolled into a ball. Durable and strong, the rope was used to make fishnets, bindings for tools, lashings for roofing and canoes and as simple household string. String used to bind food items wrapped in young coconut leaves such as billum came from fine threadlike fibers taken from the exterior of the trunks of banana trees. Tapioca is still prepared and wrapped this way today.

Pottery fragments can be found on beaches and forest floors by old village sites. The many pieces of pottery are evidence of its past abundance. Ceramic art revolved around the production of clay pots.

Pandanus mats are tough and durable. Palauans often use them to sleep on. They are also great for the beach.

layer. Fine-grained clay was mixed with sand to make potter's clay. Before kneading, the potter refired, pulverized fragments of previously baked clay. The final mixture was then combined with fresh clay, soaked in water and molded into clods that were then kneaded by hand on a straw mat. Finally the clods were pounded flat with a wooden tool shaped like a tobacco smoking pipe *(olechotech er a chutem)* and rolled into long cylindrical lengths of the desired diameter.

The creative mind of a Kayangel artist turns these water catchment basins into a thing of beauty.

Palauans did not have a potter's wheel but constructed their pottery by coiling the rounded lengths of rolled clay in an upward spiral using their hands to smooth and preliminarily shape the vessel. As construction progressed, the potter pressed and hardened the pot by beating the outside with a dual purpose pounding tool called *"brotech"* which was essentially a club that could be, and was, used in war. To absorb the shock and provide backing, a flat tool, called *"tktik,"* was held on the inside. When the fabrication phase was finished the thick part at the bottom was sliced off with an arc clam shell, *Barbatia reeveana,* and the pot was placed atop a large pile of firewood and heated for hours. As the wood burned, the pot settled deeper and deeper into the embers where it became red hot. It was extracted at the last minute before it turned black.

Europeans introduced metal containers to Palau. Palauans discovered that metal containers were more durable than clay containers. Eventually ceramic containers were replaced with metal ones. During the 1930's *Ngersuul* Village in *Ngchesar* was the center for production of clay tiles. Many clay pots were also produced in *Ngatpang*. After the Japanese era, the production of ceramic products declined.

A renewed interest in creating pottery with native clays occurred during the 1970's. Sandy Vitarelli, a self taught potter, made traditional pottery in her workshop at Palau High School for about 6 years (1973 to 1979.) Meanwhile Sandy's brother, David, set up a pottery shop in *Ngersuul, Ngchesar.* (David apprenticed with the famous Japanese potter, Hamada, in the village of Mashiko, Japan, for three years.) Herb Ward joined David and Sandy. The people of *Ngersuul* village worked with these potters and participated in all phases of pottery production. In 1979 these artists left Palau and ceramic arts ended once again. Maybe it's time to try again?

Palauan artists continue to create 21st century works as they pursue various art forms. Drawings, painting on canvas and cloth and photography are used extensively. Traditional tools and those of the modern age are combined to create jewelry, baskets, mats, wood works, stone works, homes and traditional *bai*. Whether it's a small pandanas basket for betelnut or a coconut

Palauan clay pot used for cooking.

Photo by Belau National Museum

basket for carrying taro from the taro patch, remnants of the past are easily recogniz-able. Jewelry, spears and tools made today are produced with

Palauan clay lamp.

metal and electric convenience but distinctly reflect the heritage and culture of this island nation. Tourism provides an economic incentive for artists. Storyboards are a popular gift for visitors. Private art collectors request reproductions of objects and paintings of the past. Major regional events exhibit artwork as part of Palau's rich cultural heritage. Annual fairs, celebrations and conferences provide opportunities to display and sell local art.

The *Belau* National Museum works with museums worldwide and has a large collection of art. The United Artists of *Belau* (UAB) is a local organization of artists who promote the preservation of traditional arts and create new art forms. (*Belau* is the original spelling of Palau.) Palauan artists link the past with their own present expressions. Contemporary artists work with native wood, shells and plants as well as introduced oils, paints, acrylics, watercolors and cloth. The *Belau* National Museum, the new Etpison Museum, the United Artists of *Belau*, *Ormuul* gift shop, the local prison and other stores are all avenues to purchase art and support our local artists.

REFERENCES

The Belau National Museum displays during 1997.
The Art of Micronesia. 1986. The University of Hawaii Art Gallery.

Gods and Religion of Palau. Collective Works of Hidikata Hisakatsu. 1995. The Saskawa Peace Foundation Tokyo Japan e-mail:spinf@spf.or.jp

A Portrait of Paradise. 1997. Mandy Thijssen-Eptison.

Some Ceramics of Palau. Hidikata Hisakatsu. Editor Thomas B. Mc Grath S.J. Micronesian Area Research Center Publication No. 2.

Olechotel Belau Cultural Treasures of Palau. 1998 Micronesian Games Cultural Information & Activities. Republic of Palau. Margo Vitarelli and Tina Rehuher.

Conversations with Clarence Kitalong, Tina Rehuher and Margo Vitarelli.

133

The Bai

The bai is the pinnacle of Palau's dynamic art and culture. The *bai* is a meeting house for chiefs and the community. Palauans have fond memories of their village *bai.* As boys and girls they went to the *bai* for big parties when guests came from another village *(klechedaol)* or during feasts for their clan *(mur).* They learned and taught Palauan dance at the *bai.* Dance groups go to other villages to perform. Palauans continue to use the *bai* to prepare for celebrations. The dancers call upon the elders to help perfect or straighten *(melamet)* the dances. Excitement fills the air as the time to celebrate draws near. More solemn events occur at the *bai.* Chiefs meet to determine who will get the next titles, to distribute money after customs and settle land matters. The life cycle of the community revolves around the *bai.*

Palauans living outside Palau bring the heart of their culture with them. Modern *bai* are in Guam and Saipan. Palauans practice dance *(matamatong)* for special events. Hawaii has no *bai,* so the Palau community gathers in the public park. Dancers meet in the park each weekend to practice before a celebration.

In Palau, the physical structure of most *bai* changed with time. The daily functions of the *bai* shifted to new places like schools, auditoriums and courtrooms. Yet, even with these changes, the *bai* remains the center of each village community. The roots of Palauan culture stem from the *bai.*

A dreamy timelessness fills a *bai.* Upon entry your mind becomes a dynamic haze of past and present. The past becomes the present. The present becomes the past. A *bai* is a meeting house that serves as a conference room, courtroom, library, school, and center for the arts. Chiefs made important decisions and discussed strategies in the *bai.* The beams and walls continue to be both a village library and a showcase of art. Historians recite legends of past heroes, wars and great events. Men learn about their village history. Leaders, warriors, fishermen and hunters learn necessary skills within the *bai* and the canoe house *(diangel).* Village groups learned song *(kesols)* and dance *(matematong)* at the *bai.*

A heroic demi-god called *Orachel* learned how to build the first *bai* from the gods. Once upon a time, *Orachel* was sailing home from a feast in *Angaur.* He heard a noise under

Master builder, Tabo Ngiramengior begins his work deep in the forest where large trees are cut and shaped. Traditionally, a *bai* was completely assembled in the forest near where the wood was cut. It was then taken apart and reassembled at its final location.

the sea. He dove underwater to see what was causing the noise. He saw gods building a magnificent *bai* beneath the sea. *Orachel* noticed the gods stopped frequently to

Palauan craftsman carries his *"chebakl"* over his shoulder in the traditional fashion of his ancestors. This tool is used for fitting and shaping the wooden pieces of the *bai.*

wipe from their eyes the small particles they chipped from the stone. He told the gods that he would show them how to avoid getting particles in their eyes if they taught him how to build a *bai.* The gods agreed. *Orachel* told the god to simply close their eyes before blowing the powder out of the stone holes they made. The gods did what he said and no longer needed to wipe their eyes. In return for his advice, the gods kept their promise and taught *Orachel* how to build a *bai. Orachel* became a great builder of many *bai.* He sold his first *bai* to the elders of *Aimeliik,* led by Chief *Secharemidal. Orachel* renamed him Chief *Rengulbai. Orachel* created the famous rock paintings of *Ulong* called *Ursel Orachel* (*omurs* translates "to draw")

thus The Drawings of *Orachel. Orachel* did the initial ornamentation of the canoe house *(diangel). Orachel* continued to create and build throughout his life. Then, one day, *Orachel* turned into stone off a point at *Ngatpang.* We can still find this famous mushroom shaped stone called *"Orachl'l Bad"* in *Ngatpang's* reef.

Village chiefs requested master builders of a neighboring village to build a new *bai.* It was uncustomary for a master builder to build a *bai* in his own village. The chiefs must exchange money with another village or their pride is tarnished. The chiefs' payment to a master builder is complex. The top four ranking chiefs buy the four corners of the *bai.* The fifth ranking chief buys the ridgepole. The sixth ranking chief buys two rows of thatch section including the foundation floor and walls under that section of thatch. The seventh ranking chief helps with the payment made by the sixth ranking chief. The eighth ranking chief helps the seventh ranking chief.

Basic structure of the *bai* is in place. No nails are used. Wooden members are fitted and joined like pieces of a puzzle. Roofing components are lashed together with coconut fiber rope.

The ninth ranking chief helps the first ranking chief. The tenth ranking chief helps the second ranking chief. The eleventh through to the twentieth ranking chiefs buy the remainder of the *bai.* During war time, a village could acquire a *bai* by conquering another village in battle. The victorious village disassembled the *bai's* interlocking

wooden frame and brought each piece back to their village. The number of *bai* in a village depended upon the amount of money the chiefs could spend. Some villages

Roofing for the *bai* is made from *Nypa* palm leaves sewn on bamboo batons. The batons are then assembled in an overlapping fashion that sheds water. Over 4000 bamboo and palm leaf batons were needed to make the roof of the Koror *bai*.

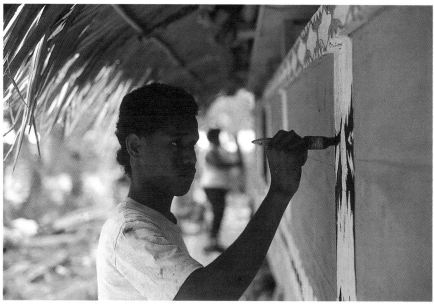

Young Palauan artist paints figures on the outside of the *bai*.

had many *bai*.

A well-built *bai* can last more than fifty years. Builders replace the roof and rafters from time to time. The master builder *(dachelbai)* supervises the construction of a *bai*, a

ritualistic and complex process. The master builder ensures the favor of the gods and spirits. He oversees the entire construction process; from the felling of the first tree (which is an omen) to the final exorcism of evil spirits. The *dachelbai* knows exactly how to construct the *bai*. Builders use a variety of woods to build different parts of the *bai*. The builder makes the floor with a hardwood, *Intsia bijuga (dort)*, found on limestone islands. Trees made of strong wood for flooring are *Calophyllum inophyllum (btaches)*, *Serianthes kanehirae* (*ukall*) and *Pterocarpus indicus (las)*. The builders make the beams with the wood of the large endemic tree *Serianthes kanehirae (ukall)*. They use the mangrove tree *Lumnitzera littorea (mekekad)* for other parts of the *bai*. They make the thatched roof with *Nypa* palm, *Nypa fruticans (toechel)*.

Builders roll up the fibers from the tree, *Hibiscus tiliaceous (chermall)* into a giant ball and use it as rope. They use coconut fiber rope to tie wooden roof rafters together and attach *Nypa* palms to the rafters. Master builders constructed traditional *bai* without metal nails. The master builder's main tool is an adze *(chebakl)*. This axe-like tool had a wooden handle and an arched blade made from a piece of a giant clam shell.

138

Traditionally, a *bai* was built on a stone platform and supported by large stones that elevated the structure and allowed air to circulate beneath the floor thus relieving dampness. A typical *bai* was about 60-feet in length, 30-feet wide and rose to a height of 40-feet. Some *bai* were wider *(meteu el bai)* with large openings for improved air circulation. Other *bai* were double the normal width. Some *bai* were two stories high. Twin *bai* were common in the past. The elderly chiefs sat in one *bai* and the younger men of high clan sat in the other. Today there are fewer traditional *bai* and the architecture is similar among them. *Bai* roofs are steep sloped and end in gables decorated with intricate paintings. (A gable is a vertical triangular upper part of wall at the end of a ridged roof.) The *bai's* interior consists of a large rectangular room with two fire pits. Side walls are of socket and

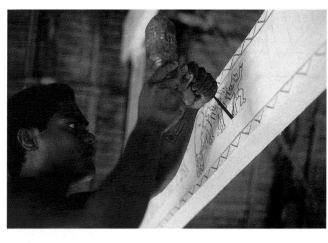

Carvings on interior rafters illustrate Palauan traditions, legends and events of historic significance.

One of two fire pits in the Koror *bai*. Fires were maintained almost continuously so that the smoke would cure the roofing leaves and keep the insects at bay. Fires were seldom used for cooking.

peg construction. The walls do not reach the thatched roof, allowing an opening for light and ventilation.

There are two types of *bai,* the chiefs' *bai (bai ra rubak)* and community or clubhouse *bai (bai ra cheldebechel).* Palauans used the community *bai* for ceremonial purposes and as a temporary home for visitors from another village. The community *bai* is a sleeping house for young unmarried men. Some *bai* had decorated wooden gables *(tetib el bai).* Other less grandiose *bai* had thatched gables *(keldok el bai).* The chiefs' *bai* is more elaborate, with decorations on the exterior and interior. Intricately carved gables, walls and interior beams adorn the chief's *bai.* The club house has a gable end and wall made of thatch and no interior decoration. In their form, decoration and construction, *bai*

Carving on the cross member in the *Aimeliik bai* relates the Palauan legend *"Bersoech ra Chelechui,"* a story about an old woman whose two sons defeat the monster that has been destroying their village.

Carvings on the interior cross members of the *bai* in Melekeok. Lightning like symbols extending from the mouths of the figures indicate speech. The bigger the lightning, the more forceful the speech.

carved or painted pictures on the crossbeams *(imuul)* that hold a *bai* together. Palauans learned their heritage through each story. A village historian describes the names and relationships between village ancestors in minute detail. Village historians sit for hours explaining the legends on each crossbeam.

One of my favorite experiences was at a *bai* in *Ngkeklau* during 1995. (The *bai* is not located at the traditional *bai* site, but closer to the pier.) *Ngkeklau* is an isolated and remote village in *Ngaraard.* Until recently, this village had no roads linking it to other villages. A large red sun radiates red light beams over the entrance door. The door faces East towards the pier. The *Ngkeklau bai* is a simple open structure with crossbeams filled with simply painted legends. My friend Linda Subris asked her village storyteller to explain some of the legends. The storyteller spent two hours telling us just four of the

are unique. The closest resemblance to a *bai* is an Indonesian building called a "bale" or *"balai."*

Local legends were carved on the rafters and beams of the village *bai* as well as famous stories from other villages. (For example the *Dilukai of Ngatpang.*) Artists painted the crossbeams of the *bai* with pictorial stories of triumphs, tragedies and important events and people. Palauans call pictures that tell a story *"lochukle."* Artists

The spider motif is found in every *bai* in Palau. It is the symbol of natural childbirth in Palauan mythology.

legends painted on the beams. His detailed knowledge of each legend amazed me. I could spend days in the *bai* listening to his fascinating stories. That afternoon in *Ngkeklau* gave me a deeper appreciation of *bai* art.

Bai art has similar themes painted in various styles by

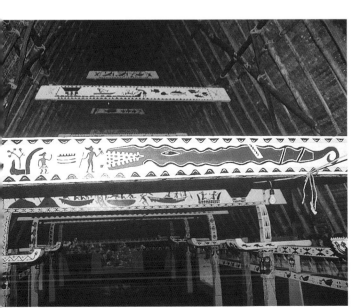

past and present artists. Artists first draw an outline of their art with black charcoal. Once an artist outlines a story on a beam, he fills it in with white paint. He makes the white paint by mixing *Calophyllum inophyllum (btaches)* leaves with water and a bundle of chalk. Artists get their colors for paint from ochre, lime, charcoal and

Roosters were common symbols carved on the bai. Village elders residing in the bai depended on the rooster to awaken them early for special occassions and events.

the red oil base extracted from the fruit of *Parinari laurina (cheritem)*. Ochre is a mixture of clay and iron with pigments of light yellow, deep orange and brown. Red pigment comes from clay. Black comes from charcoal and the ink sacs of squid.

Each *bai* is decorated with stories and motifs selected by the village chiefs. The scenes are drawn from left to right characterizing important events of the past, clan history and mythology. Stories are drawn in great detail, carved in low relief and then painted. Figures of men, women, spirits, animals, plants and other familiar objects are used to tell the tales. The storyteller brings the images to life as he weaves his tale. All eyes move slowly across the beam as he speaks. The themes revolve around romance and the

"Delerrok," mythical bird that gave birth to Palauan money. Found at all four corners of the Airai bai. It is supposed to bring good fortune to the village.

war. Romance revolved around lovers torn apart and consequences of love, such as jealousy, death and transformation into new life forms. War chronicles of famous battles between villages and warriors with clever skills of deception and fighting adorn the beams. Legends instruct the youth about their history, tradition and morals.

Popular motifs are symbols of money. Artists paint money beads, money birds and demigods with currency on the *bai*. Palauans portray the money bird as the whimbrel, *Numenius phaeopus (okak)*, a mythical currency bird *(delerrok)*. Palauan money beads consist of polychrome and clear glass of unknown origin. The most valued money bead is a yellow, crescent shaped polychrome bead called *"bachel brrak."* Money exchange was a vital part of Palauan custom. Chiefs exchanged money as a result of war reparation, punishment, marriage, heroic acts and as rewards for good service by a clan or individual.

Palauans associate the rooster and the sun *(cheos)* with the mythological creation of the first *bai*. Once upon at time, a demigod craftsman named *Kladaelbai* was working beneath the sea on parts for the first *bai*. Two other gods, *Uchel Kebesadel* and *Iechadrengel*, worked with *Kladaelbai*. They began to argue over who would control the building enterprise. *Uchel* charred some coconut fibers and tossed them into the air. A rooster appeared and began to crow. At the seventh crow *Iechadrengel*, *Uchel's* rival, thrust out the sun (which he had previously carved) and daylight flooded the islands. The gods never completed the first *bai* because they only worked at night. The rooster also

symbolizes an industrious person, who rises early and accomplishes much in a day. Palauans paint many motifs of the rooster and sun on their bai.

Painted trophy heads symbolize the triumphs of war. Palauans use motifs to symbolize cosmic renewal and placation of ancestors. Animal and marine life motifs (the eel, octopus, snake, fish, crab, rat, centipede, hawksbill turtle,

Melekeok bai east gable carving of the legendary figure of "Dilukai," the symbol of fertility.

bird and stingray) represent gods and goddesses for different Palauan villages. A border design of clam shells *(kim)* signifies the first birth of Palauans from the giant clam. Palauans eat the tasty giant clam meat and make tools and jewelry with its shell. Motifs of the famous demigod *Mengidabrudkoel* symbolize the discovery of natural birth. Two malevolent gods, *Melech* and *Olik,* decorate the *bai. Melech* took the form of a human mask with disheveled hair and a beard. Chiefs chanted to *Melech* to drive away evil spirits. Palauans captured the giant bat *Olik.* It became their guardian against evil spirits. The giant bat god *Olik* is painted on the underside of the entrance to the bai reminding those who enter to bend down as a sign of respect to the chiefs.

The most famous motif is the woman *Dilukai* who has become the symbol of fertility. Legends of *Dilukai* vary from village to village.

Stone platforms, called *"iliud,"* are situated adjacent to the main *bai* in each village. When a difficult problem could not be solved in the *bai,* the four highest chiefs adjourned to this platform to negotiate a compromise.

The *Ngatpang* version is as follows: Once upon a time a young mother named *Dilukai* was not staying home with her baby. Her brother *Bagei* became angry because she was not being a good mother. He chased her and threatened her with his spear. She ran to the chief's *bai*. One clever chief saw that she was in danger. He grabbed her, quickly pulled up her grass skirt and spread her legs apart towards her brother. The stunned brother

Europe. The Metropolitan Museum of Art in New York displays artwork from around the world. A wooden statue

Faces carved and painted on the posts of the *bai* signified "*Chedechuul*," mythical Palauan god of construction. The shelf extending out from the post was used to store bedding.

Stories carved on the cross members of the *Koror bai* are taken from all of Palau from the Southwest Islands to *Kayangel*.

quickly ran away. (A brother must not see under his sister's skirt.) The clever chief saved *Dilukai's* life at the risk of his own. This legend of *Ngatpang* became famous. The wooden statue of *Dilukai* originally adorned only the *Ngatpang bai* and *Ngeremlengui bai*. Later it became a popular motif in the center of community *bai* gables. Europeans took parts of a deteriorated *bai* from *Ngeremlengui* to Germany. These pieces of *bai*, especially the symbolic *Dilukai*, became well known in

While the faces painted on interior posts of the *Airai bai* differ from those in the *Koror bai*, the unmistakable earrings of upper mid rank Palauan money called "*chelebucheb*" identify him as "*Chedechuul*," the god of construction.

of *Dilukai* was the only item displayed for Palau during my last visit.

The motif of *Dilukai* has created much intrigue. Elders believe the legend of *Dilukai* originally focused upon the clever Chief that saved *Dilukai*. My husband, Clarence Kitalong, thinks the legend of *Dilukai* is symbolic of the strength of chiefs. A ranking chief determined *Dilukai's* fate rather than her blood relative, *Bagei*. Some believe *Dilukai* wards off evil spirits. In the past some gable boards had painted images of men with enormous penises pointed toward *Dilukai*. Palauans call these planks *Bagei* (*Dilukai's* brother) in reference to married men. Most believe that *Dilukai* signifies fertility and is a carry over from the days of concubinage. Some say the *Dilukai's* posture is a reminder for women to make their presence known when approaching the men's *bai*. The mysterious *Dilukai* will always intrigue us.

The entrances of many *bai* face eastward. This orientation allows the rays of the rising sun to enter each morning. (Some say this was an introduced concept, because old stone platforms of *bai* do not all face east-

The Koror *bai* was rebuilt in 1991.

Offerings to "*Melech*," mythical god of misfortune during opening ceremonies for the Koror *bai*. Chanting will continue all night until *Melech* is lured out of the *bai* at sunup.

ward.) The chief's *bai* was the most prominent and prestigious structure in the village. Twin *bai* were built side by side. Each village has a council of chiefs *(klobak)* that run the affairs of the villages. Ten ranking chiefs usually composed the council. Some villages have twenty chiefs.

Outside the *bai* a platform with smooth stones at the corners serves as seats for the highest chiefs. Within the *bai,* the highest chiefs sit at the four corner posts. Other chiefs sit opposite each other along the long sides of the *bai.* The two sides are opposing each other. The first and second ranking chiefs occupy the two posts under the front gable. At specific sites outside the *bai* there are special upright stones that represent the village gods and a stone offering bowl for the gods. Stones represented gods and spirits. These sacred areas received village offerings. These stones also served a more practical purpose. In *Airai* men used a large upright stone by the *bai* to brace somebody for beheading after committing a serious offense.

The physical layout and landscape of a village provides a sense of organization. Some villages had six *bai* arranged in two groups of three. They ranked these *bai* as junior,

middle and senior. Palauans built some villages that were divided down the middle by a stream or footpath. The division may have been symbolic rather than a physical division. Six *bai* represented the corner posts supporting the entire village. Villages maintained the stone foundations and special stones associated with the *bai* as well as the stone paths. The village of *Imeungs (Beluu ra Imeungs)* in *Ngeremlengui* is an important historic site and a good example of the layout of a traditional village. A stone path leads from the home sites of the four top clans to the *bai.* The stone path continues uphill to a spiritual and historic site. The stones of the path are smooth from wear and covered with moss. The Division of Cultural Affairs made a map of the site to guide visitors along the stone path.

along the way. Foundation stones mark the site of the *bai.* Betel nut palm trees, a few large *Serianthes kanehirae*

Opening ceremonies include dancing and feasts and visits by many chiefs and dignitaries.

The northern village of *Chelab* in *Ngaraard* has one of the most complete systems of stone paths in Palau. You can walk along these paths for hours

(*ukall*), fruit trees, ferns and orchids line the paths. In many villages there are old stone foundations of home

and never cross the same spot twice. There are large slabs of dark volcanic rock that serve as bridges over streams. Sometimes naked women sat on top of these large slabs to give men extra stamina to travel long distances. Large mango trees provide shade at resting points

The *Airai bai* is over 200 years old and is still in use on a regular basis. It was dismantled and stored at the beginning of WWII and put back together at the war's conclusion.

sites. In some villages Palauans built new homes on top of old stone foundations.

The records of early Europeans describe the *bai* as common and well maintained. In 1910 an anthropologist named Dr. Augustin Krämer did extensive studies of Palau. He recorded

original stories from the crossbeams of more than one hundred *bai*. Dr. Krämer found many *bai* abandoned or in deteriorating condition. The population in Palau dropped drastically by this time as a result of introduced diseases. During World War II soldiers bombed many *bai*. By 1954, there were eight traditional *bai* left in Palau. Palauans used large Quonset huts as *bai* during the 1950's. Wooden structures were replaced with steel and concrete and while some were painted with the legends of the past, some were not. Fast construction took precedent over craftsmanship. The demand for craftsmanship and skills of woodwork declined. Asphalt and concrete roads replaced many stone paths. Many of the stone paths and old villages on *Angaur* and Peleliu were destroyed during WWII. Stone paths in other parts of Palau, having lost their function, are deteriorating with time. Today, the traditional village layout of Koror

Dress rehearsal. A dance group made up of elementary school girls practice for an upcoming event under the watchful eye of village elders. Both teachers and dancers are voluntary participants.

continues to change as a result of steady development. Homes now stand over old stone paths. Newly constructed roads no longer lead to a *bai* and often cover old paths.

In 1991 concern over the future of the traditional *bai* prompted the chiefs of Koror into action. The master builders of *Ngeremlengui* were recruited to rebuild a traditional *bai* on the grounds of the *Belau* National Museum. The *bai* is called *bai ra ngeschel a cherechar*. The name of the *bai* refers to the proverb: "The past determines the present and future." This *bai* represents all of Palau. The legends carved and painted on its cross members and beams come from all over Palau, from the Southwest Islands in the south to *Kayangel* atoll in the north. Palauans reconstructed two more *bai ra rubak* or chief's *bai,* under the supervision of traditional artisans. In 1992 craftsman rebuilt the *bailekeong* or *Melekeok bai* in four months. In

Meeting held in *Airai bai* as Department of Cultural Affairs official historian records information given by village elder.

1995, artisans reconstructed the *"baingerkeai"* or the *Aimeliik bai.* There is hope that all States will eventually reconstruct their traditional *bai.*

My first experience inside a *bai* was during an induction ceremony of my Peace Corps group in 1977. The village chiefs held the ceremony at the community *bai (bai ra ngesechel a cherechar)* at the *Belau* National Museum. The Paramount Chief of Koror, Chief *Ibedul,* presided. I consciously tried to sit properly, keep still and not shift around too much. Each of us sat along the walls, still, quiet and attentive. I recalled our cultural classes about the *bai* and tried to apply what I learned. I looked with curiosity at the paintings on the beams. Legends told through art. The architecture of the building was unique. The beams fit together perfectly. There were open fire pits in the center of the floor. Each time I bring a visitor to the Koror *bai* I recall my induction day.

The oldest standing *bai* in Palau is in *Airai.* Built over 200 years ago it has undergone periodic repair. In 1910, the community replaced many of the interior beams and rafters and less durable portions were reconstructed in 1974. Repair and replacement of the roof is an ongoing community project. The entire structure was dissembled prior to WWII, placed in storage and reassembled after the war. You can drive to *Airai* village and park at the beginning of a stone path that leads to the *bai.* There are a few homes along the path. The stone path was once the main street of the village with homes lining either side. Today stone platforms are all that remain of the homes that once stood. The Chiefs of *Airai* request a fee to visit and photograph the *Airai bai.* This fee helps maintain and safeguard *Airai's* treasure.

The architecture, artwork and surrounding landscape of

Melekeok bai.

the *Airai bai* is striking. Once near the *bai* you begin to focus on the detailed art of the outer *bai.* At the top of the front entrance, there is a painted demigod with earrings of the currency symbol. A pattern of *Tridacna* clams *(kim)* borders the roof beams. The recessed gable beam has one pictorial legend. Zigzag lines border the beams with hanging currency symbols. The doorposts have painted faces of currency gods or leading women. The chiefs dedicated the posts to these women. Below the faces are clams, roosters and a border of the currency symbol. The entire structure sits on a stone platform *(oldesongel).* With special permission you can enter the *bai.* Within the *bai* the rich display of art and architecture is overwhelming. The *Airai bai* is one of Palau's special treasures and a tribute to the endurance of an art form.

I visited the site of the *Melekeok's bai (bailekeong)* before its reconstruction. It was a long beautiful walk, beginning at the pier by *Melekeok* State House. Once I reached the grounds I saw the stone platform and special upright stones on the corners and in front. I tried to imagine how the *bai* looked long ago. When the builders finished I revisited *Melekeok.* Kathy Kesolei hosted our group for the weekend. Kathy led us along a different stone path

that passes the taro patch of Chief *Reklai*. Kathy explained that Chief *Reklai* eats taro from his own taro patch. When Chief *Reklai* travels his wife brings taro for him as well as his serving dishes. Once past the taro patches we entered a large forest. Huge trees shaded the path leading to the new *bai*. Kathy received special permission from Chief *Reklai* for us to enter. Once within the *bai* we sat along the walls and listened while Kathy explained the interior features of the *bai* and legends of *Melekeok*. She explained some of the rituals required in order to become Chief *Reklai*.

After our tour we walked down a different stone path that led to the pier. Meanwhile the community prepared

Aimeliik bai is the newest Palauan *bai*, built in 1995.

a traditional feast at *Melekeok's* Senior Citizen Center. That evening Kathy graciously explained the different traditional dishes of fish and taro. Chief *Reklai*, the Governor of *Melekeok* and the community hosted a magnificent feast. After dinner Chief *Reklai* chatted with us. We all felt very special.

Bai construction instills the value of community effort. I passed by the site of the traditional *Aimeliik bai (baingerkeai)* several times during its reconstruction. Everyone worked together. The visiting builders and laborers lived in temporary shelters and in the village. *Aimeliik* women and children brought food to the work site. Palauans shared their knowledge of traditional skills to plan, design and build. Building a *bai* involves the exchange of money for skills and labor, an integral part of Palauan life.

I visited the *Aimeliik bai (baingerkeai)* after its completion. Once over the threshold a dreamy timelessness set in once again. I gazed in awe at the art and magnificent architecture surrounding me. This is the pinnacle of Palauan art. I imagined the storyteller's joy to see the brightly painted tie beams. The traditional *bai* keeps the Palauan culture vibrant.

REFERENCES

The Art of Micronesia. 1986. The University of Hawaii Art Gallery, Honolulu, Hawaii, USA.

Collected works of Hikikata Hisakatsu. 1995. Edited by ENDO Hisashi. The Sasakawa Peace Foundation. Tokyo Japan.

McKnight, R. K. 1961. *Mnemonics in Pre- literature Palau.* Anthropological working papers. A series issued from the Office of the Staff Anthropologist. Trust Territory of the Pacific Islands, Guam, M. I.

Informal chats with Sam Adelbai, Simeon Adelbai, Tina Rehuher, Margo Vitarelli and Clarence Kitalong.

GLOSSARY

Artingal - traditional name for states of Melekeok and Ngechsar
badek - burial mat
badirt - orange blossom plant, *Cordia subcordata*
bai - the men's meeting-house
bai ra cheldebechel - the communities' clubhouse or meeting house
bai ra rubak - the chiefs' meeting house
bakelungal - the black teatfish sea cucumber, *Holothuria nobilis*
balbai - mats for guests
bangikoi - a butterfly
bduul - large tree with large pink blossom, *Barringtonia asiatica*
belochel - the Micronesian pigeon, *Ducula oceanica*
bedaoch - the black noddy bird, *Anous minutus*
beduut - the forktail rabbitfish, *Signaus argenteus*
bekai - a water bottle
bekai - the Micronesian Megapode bird, *Megapodius laperouse*
Bekeu el bangaol - the fighting mangrove tree
bengobaingukl - the common sandpiper bird *Actitis hypoleucos*
berdebed - the juvenile humphead parrotfish, *Bolbometopon muricatum*
besos - a war spear
biall - leopard shark, *Stegastoma varium*
bidekill - cast net
biib - Palauan fruit dove, *Ptilinopus pelewensis*
bilas - slow wooden boat with a four horsepower Yanmar diesel engine or equally slow boat
billum - wrapped grated tapioca
bischard - the spider lily plant, *Hymenocallis littoralis*
bisech - a wild taro plant
blacheos - a tree with purple blossoms, *Gmelina palawensis*,
blades - rope made with coconut cord
blangtalos - a type of bark used for cordage, also bannana cordage
blau - the tree, *Guettarda speciosa*
blebaol - the severed head of an enemy or victim of revenge
blilch - the Engel's mullet fish *Valamugil engeli*
bloket - a basket with large openings
bluu - seat built on a bamboo raft
bngaol - mangrove tree, *Rhizophora apiculata*
bochela uchererak - the endemic palm, *Gulubia palauensis*
boes ra ngikel - speargun for fishing
boid - a tone song
borotong - cargo canoe
brak - the large yellow taro *Alocasia macrorrhiza*
brer - a bamboo raft
brotech - wooden paddle
bruk - personal sleeping mat
brul a ngalek - babies' mats
bsukl - soldier fish, *Myripristis* spp.

btaches - the large tree, *Calophyllym inophyllym*
btuul - the tree, *Barringtonia asiatica*
buchelsechal - the women married to the men of a family
budech - the yellow-cheeked tuskfishes, *Choerodon anchorago*
buich - the tiger cowrie shell, *Cypraena tiger*
bungaruau - a rubbery vine, *Polyscias grandiflora*
buuch - the betelnut palm *Areca catechu*
buuk - plate used for taro
buuk - the *Pandanus* tree, *Pandanus kanehirae*
chai - large barracuda fish *Sphyraena barracuda*
chai - pestle for pounding, made from thick sections of giant clam shell
chaol - young milkfish *Chanos chanos*
chaus - lime used with betel nut
chebacheb - the jungle nightjar bird, *Caprimulgus indicus*
chebakl - an adze
chebeludes - a strand plant, *Allophylus timorensis*
chedeng - generic term for shark
chedoched - the silver mokarras fish *Gerres abbreviatus*
chelais - a fishing basket made of coconut leaves
chelangel - the brown leafed tree, *Pouteria obovata*
chelbucheb - a Palauan money bead that is blue with white dots
cheldebechel - men's club
cheleuocho - a large fishing basket
chelodechoel - the tree *Trema orientalis*
cheluch - coconut oil
cheludel - sail of boat made from *Pandanus* leaves
chemaidechedui - the green skink, *Lamprolepis smaragdina*
chemang - the mangrove crab, *Scylla serrata*
chemeklachel - the forest tree *Horsfieldia amklaal*
chemirchorech - small grouper fish, *Epinephelus merra*
cheos - sun
cherechur - the freshwater shrimp
cheremrum - the small black sea cucumbers *Actinopyga miliaris* and *Actinopyga echinites*
cheritem - a tree, *Paranari laurina,* the fruit is used to make paint
cheriut - grass skirt
chermall - the yellow *Hibiscus* tree, *Hibiscus tiliaceous*
cheropk - the giant trevally, *Caranx ignobilis*
chersuuch - the mahi mahi fish, *Coryphaena hippurus*
chertochet - the tree, *Pandanus aimiriikensis*
chesall - the silverfish, *Gerres oyena*
chesall - the Oyena mojarra fish, *Gerres oyena*
chesbuuch - the palm tree, *Ptychosperma palauensis*
chesechol - the white beach clam, *Atactodea* spp.
chesechol - the small white beach clam, *Atactodea* spp. used in coconut soup
chesechuul - ghost crabs *Ocypode* sp.

chesiklechol - the crescent -banded grunter fish, *Terapon jarbua*
chesisbarsech - the Palauan bush warbler, *Cettia annae*
chesisebangiau - the cardinal honeyeater bird *Myzomela cardinalis*
chesisekiaid - the small swiftlet bird, *Aerodramus vanikorensis*
chesiuch - mother-of-pearl shell, *Pteria martensii*
chesmiich - the tree, *Terminalia samoensis*
chesuch - the Palauan owl, *Pyrroglaux podargina*
chesuuch - big eye trevally, *Caranx sexfasciatus*
chibars - the fish, *Pentapodus caninus* and the spinecheeks fish, *Scolopsis* sp.
chidabl - threespot cardinalfish *Apogon trimaculatus*
chidib - a small woven container used to hold betel vine leaves
chirchocher - fish hooks
chis - shallow pools with exposed areas near shore
chisebsab - the red spiral ginger plant, *Costus sericeus*
chius - seeds
choalech - the long spined black sea urchin, *Diadema* sp.
choas - lime mineral used with betel nut
chol - beach
cholechodech - a war spear
cholechutel - a raft of more than ten bamboo used for hauling heavy loads
choshiruko - a sweet purple bean Japanese soup
chosm - a tree with clusters of tiny black berries, *Premna obtusifolia*
chudech - the yellow-line emperor fish *Lethrinus obsoletus*
chum - the blue spine unicorn fish, *Naso unicornis*
dachelbai - master builder or skilled craftsman
dait - small greyish purple taro *Colocasia esculenta*
debechel - the lemon tree *Citrus limon*
dechedech ra Belau - the endemic Palau frog, *Platymantis pelewensis*
dekel - a bamboo pole
delal a kar - a small tree, *Phaleria nisidai* called "the mother of medicine"
delerrok - a mythical currency bird
demailei - the palm tree *Pinaga insignis* or *Heterospathe elata* var. *palauensis*
denges - an oriental mangrove tree, *Bruguiera gymnorhiza*
dermetaoch - small inlet in the mangroves
deroech - the little pied cormorant bird, *Phalacrocorax melanoleucos*
desui - the rainbow runner fish, *Elagatis bipinnulatus*
diangel - the canoe house
Dilukai - a woman symbolic of fertility found on the bai.
diokang - tapioca
ditmechei - the ti plant, *Cordyline terminalis*
doko - the lantern tree, *Hernandia sonora*

dort - the hardwood tree, *Intsia bijuga*

drau - a special net with sticks that acts like a very loose scoop net

duadeb - a giant clam, *Hippopus hippopus*

dudek - the white-tailed tropic bird, *Phaethon lepturus*

dukl - the Titan trigger fish, *Balistoides viridescens*

dudurs - the beach pea plant, *Sophora tomentosa*

erangel - the orange spine unicorn fish, *Naso lituratus*

eues - the sumac tree, *Rhus taitensis*

iakkotsiang - an introduced greater sulphur Crested Cockatoo or Eclectus Parrot, *Cacatua galerita*

iaml - a small plant in the snapdragon family called *Limnophila aromatica*

iasumba - a bamboo bench

ibuchel - the short spined sea urchin, *Tripneustes gratilla*

iedel - the mango tree *Mangifera indica*

ilengel - large bowl for drinking a sweet coconut syrup mixture

imekurs - the tree, *Averrhoa bilimbi*

imuul - tie beams of the men's meeting house

irang - flowers of ylang-ylang tree, *Cananga odorata*

irimd - the sea cucumber *Stichopus* species

itotech - the blackspot emperor fish, *Lethrinus harak*

itouch - the false staghorn fern, *Gleichnia linearis*

iuetekil - the vine, *Clerodondron tompsonae*

ius - the estuarine crocodile, *Crocodylus porosus*

kabekl - war canoe

kaeb - sailing canoe

kalngebard - the cotton tree, *Ceiba pentandra*

kamarido - a tree with blue drupes or fruits- *Cerbera floribunda*

katsuo - skipjack tuna fish, *Katsuwonis pelamis*

katuu el tiau - the saddleback grouper fish, *Plectropomus laevis*

kauang - clay cooking pot

keai - a thick betel nut mat of fiber used to wrap food

keam - the tropical chestnut tree, *Inocarpus fagifer*

kebeas - vine

kebeaschol - lavender morning glory, *Ipomoea pes-carprae*

kebokeb - inner margins of the mangrove forest

kebui - the betel pepper vine, leaves of vine used with betel nut and lime

keburs - the mangrove forest

kedarm - chamber nautilus, *Nautilus* spp.

kedesau - the large red snapper fish, *Lutjanus bohar*

kedesau 'l iengel - the river snapper fish, *Lutjanus argentimaculatus*

kelalk - the black snapper fish, *Monotaxis* spp.

kelat - the bluespot mullet fish, *Moolgarda sehelis*

keldellel. the beach pea, *Vigna marina*

keldok el bai - thatched gables of the men's meeting house

kelel a charm - the tree, *Campnosperma brevipetiolata*

kelsechdui - the shrub, *Vitex negundo* var. *bicolor*

kemedukl - the humphead parrotfish, *Bolbometopon muricatum*

kemokem - the vine *Derris trifolia*

kerdeu - the "ghost" plant, *Ixora casei* that has clusters of red-orange flowers

kerdikes - sedge plant, *Eleocharis* spp.

keremlal - the red humpback snapper, *Lutjanus gibbus*

kerumes - the medicine tree, *Aidia cochincninensis*

kesiil - the Rock Island guava tree, *Eugenia reinwardtiana*

keskas - the wahoo fish, *Acanthocybium solandri*

kesokes - a set net

kesol - yellow turmeric ginger plant *Curcuma domestica*

kesols - songs

ketat - the coconut crab, *Birgus latro*

kidel - the wax apple tree, *Eugenia malaccensis*

kieu - the halfbeak fish *Hemiramphus far*

kikoi - the ark shells, *Anadara* sp. and *Barbatia* sp.

kirrai - large shore shrub, *Scaevola sericea*

kisaks - lavender flowered tree, *Pongamia pinnata*

kism - clam shell or giant clam, *Tridacna derasa*

kitelel - freshwater eel, *Anguilla marmorata*

kiud - black Micronesian starling, *Aplonis opaca*

klechedaol - parties between villages

klibiskang - single pronged spear

klilt - series of bracelets

klloiskang - special small throw spears used near the mangrove

klorwikl - the savanna shrub

klsebuul - the rabbitfish, *Siganus lineatus*,

kmai - the swimming blue reef crab, *Portunus pelagicus*

koranges - the tree *Barringtonia racemosa* found near streams, fruits used for soap

korrai - large shore shrub, *Scaevola sericea*

kotraol - sailing and paddling canoe

lalou - outer edge of the mangrove

las - a hardwood tree, *Pterocarpus indicus*, sometimes used to make canoes and *bai* flooring

lemau - blue holes of inner reef

lild - thin bamboo-like tree, *Schizostachyum lima*

lius - coconut palm tree, *Cocos nucifera*

lkes - exposed sandbar

lochukle - pictures that tell stories are called

lolou - blackfin barracuda, *Sphyraena genie*

lulk - large fig trees, *Ficus.* spp.

luut -squid including *Sepioteuthis* sp.

mahogani - the Mahogany tree, *Swietenia mahogani*

malkureomel - the domesticated red jungle rooster, *Gallus gallus*

maml - the large humphead wrasse fish, *Cheilinus undulatus*

matamatong - dance

matukeoll - the blacktip shark *Carcharhinus melanopterus*

meai - **barracuda**, *Sphyraena pinguis*

meas - the rabbitfish, *Signaus fuscescens*

mechur - the yellowlip emperor fish, *Lethrinus xanthochilus*

medal a kikoi - translates to "eyes of the clam"

mederart - grey reef shark, *Carcharhinus amblyrhynchos*

medob - the large sperm whale *Physeter catadon*

meduu - the breadfruit tree, *Artocarpus altilis*

meduulokebong, - less common cannonball tree of mangrove, *Xylocarpus granatum*

mekekad - the mangrove tree *Lumnitera littorea*

mekebud - the small herring fish, *Herklotsichthys quadrimaculatus*

melabaob - a Rufous night heron, *Nycticorax caledonicus*

melamet - elders to help perfect the dance

melangmud - long nose emperor fish, *Lethrinus elongatus*

melibes - the giant clam *Tridacna maxima*

meliik - the pitcher plant, *Nepenthes mirabilis*

melimdelebteb - the brown fantail bird, *Rhipidura lepida*

mellemau - Bleeker's parrotfish, *Scarus bleekeri*, the bullethead parrotfish, *Scarus sordidus*

melob - green turtle, *Chelonia mydas*

mengardechelucheb - the grouper fish, *Cephalopholis argus*

mengardechelucheb - the peacock grouper, *Cephalopholis argus*

mengeai - neap tide

mengereel - a fishing method in which one casts over shallow water with a light line and hook size (less than size no. 5) with an optional light weight attached

mengerengel chedeng - tiger shark, *Galeocerdo cuvier*

mengol - female entertainment

mengur- coconut at middle growth stage with sweet juice and thin meat layer

meremarech -sea cucumber *Bohadschia argus*

mesei - taro patch

meseoes -the "praying" tree, *Aglaia palauensis*

mesekelat- the milk fish, *Chanos chanos*

mesekiu - the dugong, *Dugon dugon*

mesiich - strong

mesurech - hot bath during the first birth of a child

metau - mature coconut

meteu el bai - a wide *bai*

metmut - the nurse shark, *Nebrius concolor*

miich - the tropical almond tree, *Terminalia catappa*

mirechorech - the small honeycomb grouper *Epinephelus merra*

mlai ra bul - Southwest Island canoe

modechel - the black goby fish *Bathygobius cocosensis*

molech - white sea cucumber *Holothuria scabra*

mongel - a woman who entertains

mur - big dancing party

Ngardmau

ngark - small crescent-shaped, metal scrapper

ngas - ironwood tree, *Causarina equisetifolia*

ngasech - same hawksbill turtle *Eretmochelys imbricata*

ngasech - a picturesque ceremony after the first birth

ngduul - mangrove clam, *Anodontia philippina*

ngelngal - large king mackerel fish, *Scomberomorus commerson*

Ngerukewid Islands the Rock Island Wildlife Preserve

ngesil - shore plant with yellow flowers, *Wedelia biflora*

ngidech - climbing fern, *Lygodium circinatum*

ngimer- juvenile humphead wrass, *Cheilinus undulatus*

ngimes - sea cucumber, *Stichopus variegatus*

ngis - small tree with white wrinkled petals, *Pemphis acidula*

ngyoach- the Pacific longnose parrotfish, *Hipposcarus longiceps*

odesongel - stone platform

okak - whimbrel bird, *Numenius phaeopus* moneybird symbolized on the Bai

olaod - spear to catch sardines

olbidel - clay lantern

Olbiil Era Kelulau - House of Whispers

olechodech - war spear or club

olechotech er a chutem - a wooden tool with a smoke pipe shape used to make pottery

oledabel - an elaborate wooden money jar

olekang - clay cooking pot

olik - the Palau fruit bat, *Pteropus pelewensis*

olisall - clay cooking pot

olongosall - clay cooking pot

oltall - a pot to boil coconut syrup

oltoir - a fishing method in which one watches the ripples on the surface, makes a chase and lightly races over the reef and throws a spear.

olumud - war club

omdesakl - fishing method using a heavier line and a small weight just above a large hook (size no. 6-8).

omebael - a husband's family may place this type of Palauan money on a wife when she is pregnant

omedeto - a Japanese word that translates to "congratulations"

omengades - a ceremony after the funeral when the grave is decorated with rocks or bottles.

omsangel - a basket that women store their personal effects

ongall - wooden plate to serve fish

ongedeched - a tool used to remove thorns from *Pandanus*

ongederaoll - clay cooking pot

Ongeim'l Tketau Uet - jellyfish lake on Eil Malk Island

ongelidel - small pots to boil water

ongiut - a *Pandanus* leaf splitter made with Mother of Pearl shell

ongor - the *Pandanus* trees *Pandanus dubius* and *Pandanus tectorius*

orekill - a basket to hold cooked starch

orredakl - the lily, *Dracaena multiflora* (orredakl)

orsachel - wooden bowl to pound betel nut or medicine

oruer - the giant clam imbedded into coral, *Tridacna crocea*

oruidel - bluefin trevally fish, *Caranx melampygus*

oruikl - a small basket that men store their personal effects

otilech - a type of axe

otkang - the largest giant clam, *Tridacna gigas*

otungel - the pouch inside a grass skirt

ouklemedaol - the large manta ray, *Manta alfredi*

raielchol - large shore shrub, *Scaevola sericea*

rebotel - the Palauan apple tree, *Eugenia javanica*

rekung 'l beluu - the black land crab, *Cardisoma hirtipes*

rekung 'l daob - the brown land crab, *Cardisoma carnifex*

remiang - the stout cycad plant, *Cycas circinalis*

riamel - the football tree, *Pangium edule*

ribkungel - giant clam, *Tridacna squamosa*

rirs - heliotrope tree, *Tournefortia aregentea*

roall - great crested tern bird, *Sterna bergii*

rolel a kelulau - the way of politics

roro - the catclaw tree, *Erythrina variegata* var. *orientalis*

rrull - stingrays, *Dasyastis* species

rur - the endemic white lily of the Rock Islands, *Bikkia palauensis*

ruul - a sweep net made of coconut and other palm leaves

sang - the spider shell, *Lambis lambis*

saru - thin hard vine basket

sau - the savanna grass, *Digitaria violascens*

sechou - reef heron, *Egretta sacra*

semum - the top shell gastropod, *Trochus niloticus*

sikeruo - a net of coconut or *Hibiscus* fibers tied between two bamboo poles used by one man to catch bats

sis - ti plant, *Cordyline* spp.

skobang - broom made with midrib of coconut leaves

skobetang - Palauan gun

smach - striped mackerel, *Rastrelliger kanagurta*

Taem er chelid - time of gods

taoch - the mangrove channel

taod - multipronged fish spear

tarai - metal basin

tebechel - the mangrove tree, *Rhizophora mucronata*

techellel a chull -vine *Cassytha filiformis*

tekuu - large yellowfin tuna, *Thunnus albacares*

telab - yellow ginger

temekai. -the grouper fish in the Genus *Epinephelus*.

temikel - the subsidiary rib of a coconut frond

temtamel - the prickly redfish sea cucumber, *Thelenota ananas*

tengadidik -the collared kingfisher, *Halcyon chloris*

terekrik - the scad fish, *Selar crumenophthalmus*

terir - large spoons

tet - small woven baskets with personal belongings

tetib el bai - decorated wooden gables

tiau - groupers in the Genus *Plectropomus* spp.

titimel -the tree, *Spondias pinnata*

tktik - tool to hold the inside of bot while forming it

toechel - the Nypa palm, *Nypa fruticans*

toluk - shell of an adult hawksbill is made into a small tray that is used as women's money

tonget - the poison tree, *Semecarpus venensosus*

torech - slender vine, *Ipomoea littoralis*

Towachel Mlengui - Ngeremlengui Channel

tutau - the morning bird, *Pitohui tenebrosa*

uet - pool in the mangroves

Uet ra Edead -Big Jellyfish Lake

Uet ra Utoi -Gobi Lake

ukaeb - stuffed land crabs, *Cardiosoma hirtipes* and *C. carnifex*.

ukall - a hardwood tree, *Serianthes kanehirae*

ukellel a chedib - a small plant, *Phyllanthus palauensis* used as medicine

uleiull - the outer muddy edge of the mangrove; mound

ulekelakel - a small plant in snapdragon family *Limnophila fragrans*

ulekput - a small spear for a blow gun

ulitech - an old-style hanging door hand woven with *Pandanus* leaves

uloi - an archerfish, *Toxotes jaculatrix*

uluu - the yellowtail mullet, *Ellochelon vaigiensis*

urur - the mangrove tree, *Sonneratia alba*

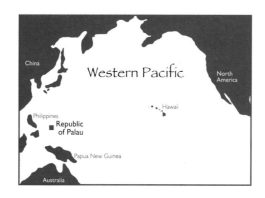

China

Western Pacific

North America

Hawaii

Philippines
Republic
of Palau

Papua New Guinea

Australia

Kayangel

Palau
Archipelago

Republic of Palau

Ngarchelong

Ngardmau

Ngaraard

Ngeremlengui

Ngiwal

Ngatpang

Melekeok

Aimeliik

Ngchesar

Koror

Airai

Southwest Islands

Fana

Sonsorol

The Southwest
Islands of Palau
are located
approximately
200 miles
southwest
of Koror.

Pulo Anna

Merir

Peleliu

Angaur